PUBLIC PRIVATES

Public Privates

Feminist Geographies of Mediated Spaces

MARCIA R. ENGLAND

UNIVERSITY OF NEBRASKA PRESS   LINCOLN AND LONDON

Portions of chapter 7 were originally published
as "Suicide Girls: Bodies, Beauty, and
Cyberspace," in *Aether: The Journal of Media
Geography* 8:137–53. Used with permission.

Library of Congress Cataloging-in-Publication Data
Names: England, Marcia R., author.
Title: Public privates: feminist geographies of
mediated spaces / Marcia R. England.
Description: Lincoln: University of Nebraska Press,
2018. | Includes bibliographical references and index. |
Identifiers: LCCN 2017036455 (print)
LCCN 2018002650 (ebook)
ISBN 9781496207333 (epub)
ISBN 9781496207340 (mobi)
ISBN 9781496207357 (pdf)
ISBN 9781496205803 (hardback)
ISBN 9781496206725 (paperback)
Subjects: LCSH: Feminist geography. | Mass media—
Social aspects. | Gender identity. | BISAC: SOCIAL
SCIENCE / Human Geography. | SOCIAL SCIENCE /
Media Studies. | SOCIAL SCIENCE / Gender Studies.
Classification: LCC HQ1233 (ebook) | LCC
HQ1233 .E545 2018 (print) | DDC 305.3—dc23
LC record available at https://lccn.loc.gov/2017036455

Set in Garamond Premier by Mikala R Kolander.
Designed by N. Putens.

This book is dedicated to the community of friends, family, and mentors who have supported me over the years and put up with my "laid forward" personality.

Contents

Acknowledgments

I would like to acknowledge the geography departments at the University of Washington, University of Kentucky, University of South Carolina, and Miami University for use of their facilities and access to their faculty over the years—specifically the faculty at the University of Washington and University of Kentucky who mentored and advised me during my undergraduate and graduate years and my colleagues at the University of South Carolina and Miami University. Thank you to the anonymous and known reviewers who have given their time to improve my work.

Introduction

Media of communication . . . are vast social metaphors that not only transmit information, but determine what is knowledge; that not only orient us to the world, but tell us what kind of world exists.
—James Carey

We live mediated lives. Media infiltrate almost every aspect of life. Experiencing media happens daily and media are a nearly constant presence at home, at work, on the streets. As such, they inform our everyday geographies. They help to code our spatial understandings of places and spaces. Media are now mobile and accessible from places they have not been before. They have new geographies—geographies that can now be seen and experienced anywhere. Geographers need to investigate further the role of the media (especially those as popular and accessible as movies, television, music, and the Internet) in the formation and construction of socio-spatial understandings. These cultural technologies influence social and spatial power relations and produce social differences and hierarchies.

This book seeks to understand the formation of geographies by focusing on public and private acts in mediated spaces. Media examination produces new understandings of geographies of public and private spaces. It sits at the intersections of cultural geography, feminist geography, and media studies. Within, I argue that media both reinforce and subvert traditional notions of public and private spaces through depiction of behaviors and actions within those spheres.

To this end, I examine the gendered representations of public and private spaces in media and how those images influence imagined and lived geographies. Feminist work in the emerging area of media geography is still relatively rare. This book makes a contribution to the field by approaching a variety of media from a feminist approach that analyzes both gender and space.

I posit that popular culture, specifically visual media, transmits ideologies that essentially disintegrate the already blurred boundaries between public and private spaces. I call this "public privates." Popular media contribute to the erosion of the indistinct edges between public and private spaces (or the process of creating public privates), yet media frequently reinforce the socially constructed separation of public and private spaces. Images emitted from screens influence both public and private spaces through particular codings, which designate the normed and gendered socio-spatial actions appropriate in each sphere. The public-private dualism and the codings within each produce geographical imaginations and behaviors.

Media Geographies

Media, as representations of space, provide opportunities to explore the social and the spatial by examining the spaces portrayed and the actions and behaviors of the characters within those spaces. Although the place depicted on a television program, movie, chat room, magazine, or video game may not exist in reality, it is given ontological status through its representation. It becomes real as it is viewed and becomes part of the viewer's geographical imagination. Lukasz Plesnar argues that "represented space has . . . all formal properties of physical space and its relations to the world of represented events is the same as that of physical space to the world of physical events."[1] Media are an essential component in the formation of individual and social experiences and how people understand public and private spaces. Popular culture, in general, plays a substantial role in how we comprehend the world around us, whether it be immediate surroundings and situations or those more distant.

Academic research sometimes classifies popular media (such as television) as low culture and thus disregards it, which negates its power as a force that creates cultural identities. But media help to shape and form identities by playing a meaning-making role in the formation of the social self. Media influence how the audience perceives themselves, others, and the spaces around them. One's identity informs how a message is interpreted; yet the message can also inform one's identity. For Sonia Livingstone, "Media cultures provide not only interpretive frameworks, but also sources of pleasure and resources for identity-formation which ensure that individuals certainly have a complex identity of which part includes their participatory relations with particular media forms."[2]

Media influence the shaping of today's culture and social roles. Ideas about who we are, what we should do, what we should look like, and what we should buy flash at us every time we experience mediated images and messages. Media's power centers on its omnipresence in society and the influence this ubiquity can have upon the behaviors and identities of both the individual and society as a whole. Media shape not only our perceptions of reality, but also our relations with one another. They provide a template on how to act according to one's role and setting.[3] Douglas Kellner observes: "Media stories provide the symbols, myths and resources through which we constitute a common culture and through the appropriation of which we insert ourselves into this culture. Media spectacles demonstrate who has the power and who is powerless, who is allowed to exercise force and violence and who is not."[4] Ever-present within modern life, media promote ideological discourses in a subtle and repetitive manner.[5] The inherent problem in these distributions of ideas is that media can be read as naturalizing ideologies instead of as constructs.[6] Images of social relations and the spaces in which these processes take place affect the viewer and—through repetitive reinforcement—they legitimize the coding of spaces and constructions of identity. Stuart Hall argues:

Media's main sphere of operations is the production and transformation of ideologies. . . . Ideologies produce different forms of social consciousness, rather than being produced by them. They work most effectively when we are not aware that how we formulate and construct a statement about the world is underpinned by ideological premises; when our formations seem to be simply descriptive statements of how things are (i.e., must be), or of what we can 'take-for-granted.' . . . In modern societies, the different media are especially important sites for the production, reproduction, and transformation of ideologies. . . . But institutions like the media are peculiarly central to the matter since they are, by definition, part of the dominant means of ideological production.[7]

For example, media portrayal of everyday occurrences creates the illusion that it is a reflection of everyday life, of how things in the world work, instead of a reflection of someone's idea of how the world works. For Phillip Green, "When ideological discourse 'works,' it does so by . . . seeming to be just a believable story about real people and their lives. Whatever social roles are eventually to receive us, visual culture is capable of presenting these roles as natural."[8] Ideologies about who we are or how we should act appear naturalized, not artificial, not as manifestations of power and social control. They do not appear as social constructions, but rather as how things are "supposed"' to be (for example, ideologies that state it is "natural" for girls to play with dolls instead of acknowledging the role of social conditioning). Many times, audiences interpret representations within media as reality instead of a construct. This can lead to what John Fiske describes as a blurred distinction between reel and real that hides the staged and performed aspects.[9] Furthermore, these performed actions seem to be objective representations of reality.

Gender roles are no exception to this rule. John Corner discusses how television works in this manner by arguing that it manipulates gender discourses and inequalities in such a way that it uncritically perpetuates patriarchy.[10] Media construction of certain stereotypes reinforces gendered social relations by creating idealized images that influence identity and gender roles within the audience.

Virtual Affectivity

Affectivity is another way through which to explore media texts. Through the framework of virtual affectivity, I discuss how virtual aspects of space allow for new explorations of geographies.[11] Virtual affectivity affects the overarching theme of public privates by demonstrating how the visual and virtual (publics, in the case of the book) affect the body/viewer (privates, in one sense of how I use "private space" within). James Craine argues that "the virtual is necessarily an element of the very body which it serves to constitute *because* the virtual is indeed an essential part of the determination of the geographies of every concrete biocultural body."[12] Spaces and places become "known" to the readers of media texts because of their virtual participation.[13] Real experiences affect the reel world of the viewers as well as the reverse. Virtual spaces can be liberating as they provide for new interpretations of places, identities, and experiences.

Virtual experiences lead to what Craine states as the relationship between the virtual environment and the body: "This engagement provides the biological self with the means to compensate for the loss of the corporeal in the virtual environment—the viewer/consumer can now simply transform that environment into a space more susceptible to human control. Thus the virtual digital environment becomes a fundamental part of human experience—there is a literal projection of the human into virtual space thereby allowing the viewer/ consumer to construct a spatial simulacrum of the previously invisible circulation of information through this simultaneous grounding and dislocating of the viewer/consumer's bodily experience."[14] This allows for an experience that can reify and destabilize conceptions surrounding public and private spaces. As media are geographical sites, we experience them with our bodies and emotions (which, of course, are also corporeal processes). That is the only way we can experience them, yet they can also be a way of divorcing spaces and bodies. Vivian Sobchack states: "Electronic space constructs objective and superficial equivalents to depth, texture, and invested bodily movement . . . constant action and 'busyness' replace the gravity which grounds and orients the movement of the lived body with a purely spectacular, kinetically exciting, and often dizzying, sense of bodily freedom."[15]

Drawing on Henri Bergson and Gilbert Simondon, Mark B. N. Hansen discusses how these philosophers conceptualized and theorized the role of affect in perceptual and sensory experience.[16] Hansen details how Bergson argued that affect and perception are intrinsically linked: "Every act of perceiving an object (or image) at a distance from one's body (or literally, as the potential for the body to act on that object) is necessarily accompanied by an action of the body on itself, a self-affection of the body."[17]

Gendered bodies can be an important component of affect. There is a patriarchal construction of female bodies as more susceptible or more closely linked to affect. Yet, as discussed above, virtual spaces can both reinforce and subvert gendered bodies and norms.

Mediating Gender

Geography is key to understanding gender identity because individuals, societies, and places are gendered. Space is not neutral, although it may seem as if it is. Gendered identities play out in both public and private spaces. Gendered ideals form gendered spaces both on the screen and within reality (the reel/real dichotomy) through the portrayal and legitimization of gendered social relations. Gendered constructions of identity and gendered codings of space are not static and have the potential for flux. Many of the examples used within this book show how gendered stereotypes can be reified, disrupted, or both.

Many monumental moments in media have transformed and undermined traditional gendered frameworks, such as shows with female lead characters who work or lead characters with nontraditional families or lifestyles. Despite moments of subversiveness, media often reproduce the traditional structuring of public and private spaces.[18] The gendering of space created by characters, their interactions, and the coded spaces they produce through these interactions reinforces these structures. The danger of many media images comes from their legitimization of gendered structures and stereotypes. Television and movies bombard audiences with images of how we as a gendered society are supposed to act in space.[19] Martyn Youngs states: "Because television looks like reality, people assume it is reality."[20] Media continually reinforce the framework that there are gendered roles for people to follow. It is as if there are formulae for how men and women should act within private and public spaces. These blueprints of gender manifest in the formation of mental maps that affect everyday geographies and social relations.

Media play powerful ideological roles through their depiction of society regardless of whether the society portrayed is fictional or not. Media can reinforce and subvert social norms, create gendered identities, and form geographical imaginations. These topics are alive and well in current academic debate, yet the connections between media, ideology, and geography are not necessarily explored as a network of societal norming.

Public Privates

Public space has long been defined as masculine and was defined as such throughout Western history because men (typically white, privileged men) were the only ones allowed to participate in public policy and actions.[21] Historically these men—since the times of the ancient Greeks—exclusively had the power to influence their environment, both physically (land ownership) and socially (the right to vote in democratic societies). Relations between the sexes and between gendered ideals of behavior (active=male=public, while passive=female=private) throughout time have defined the public as masculine and the private as feminine.[22] Definitions and divisions have been used to shape gendered relations and to define gendered ideals of behavior.

Since spaces are socially constructed and imagined, they differ cross-culturally. As such, my discussion of public and private space is predicated on Western conceptions.[23] The notion of public space, when used in this book, refers to those spaces that the public at large can readily access. These include streets, sidewalks, alleyways, parks, schools, and businesses. Although I acknowledge that some of the above could be described as private property due to the privatization of public spaces, the important aspect in my definition of public space is that of access. The above places are open to the public, albeit sometimes conditionally (e.g., hours of operation).

I describe private space as spaces that are primarily residential or intimate. Once again, I acknowledge that many nonresidential spaces are considered private property, but for all intents and purposes, I define private spaces as residences. This definition is expanded to understanding that the body is also a private and intimate space. The body is also a public surface, but for this book, it is a private space.

Bodies and portrayals of the body are important to analyze because of the history of social constructions placed on the body. Following anthropologist Mary Douglas, Steve Pile argues that "the contours of the body are the contours of society."[24] Scholars who seek to disrupt the naturalization of the body question how constructions of the body relate to other social constructions, but it is important to acknowledge just whose bodies are being portrayed and the ramifications of those representations.

While the body is also a public representation, it is the most intimate of geographical sites. Geographical analysis of the body is important because the body functions as the most personal of scales. The site of the body provides intimate understandings of geographical processes. The body is socially constructed and, as such, needs to continue to be investigated geographically. Geographers explore the body in a variety of ways ranging from the body in theory to empirics on the body.[25] Studies of the body and of representations of the body are significant to geography and geographers because of the struggle over depictions of the body and what that means to culture. Teresa de Lauretis argues that "the stakes, for women, are rooted in the body."[26] Gillian Rose furthers this argument by recalling the feminist slogan "Your body is a battleground."[27] The body, including its definitions and portrayals, is a prominent field in geography because investigations of bodies lead to examinations of social and cultural norms.

These norms feed into definitions of what is public and what is private. Public and private are imbricated concepts. A strict division between the two is not possible as the two are linked to one another.[28] While some distinctions exist between public and private space, increasingly the boundaries blur.

Methodology

The methodological approach of this book is to discuss mediated experiences as texts rather than as genre pieces, although many of these texts fit into the genres in which they are often positioned. Examining each as a mediated text provides for flexibility within my analysis and does not constrain me to discuss the piece in the light of conventional guidelines outlined by genres. I ask two primary questions: What geographical narratives do these texts exhibit? What can these narratives tell us about the way society conceptualizes gendered public and privates spaces?

The representations examined serve as empirical examples of mediated constructions of geographies. Rosalyn Deutsche argues that "representations are not objects at all, but social relations, themselves productive of meaning and subjectivity."[29]

I base my exploration of the representations of public and private spaces within media texts on textual, visual, and discourse analysis of the images and dialogue. This process of analyzing visual codes involves viewer bias.[30] In my notes, I listed spaces I interpreted to be private and described the action(s) that took place within that space, doing the same for public spaces. I differentiated between public and private space by designating public spaces as those spaces to which people have a reasonable degree of accessibility, meaning that there are no overt restrictions on one's presence. Private spaces were labeled as residential or as the site of the body. Shirley Ardener, Liz Bondi, Nancy Duncan, Ted Kilian, Linda McDowell, Gillian Rose, and Daphne Spain influenced definitions of the distinction between public and private spaces.[31]

Outline of the Book

This book examines visual media to highlight how mediated public and private spaces depict, uphold, and/or collapse constructed distinctions between public and private space. Chapters are not organized according to type of media, but instead around codings of public and private spaces.

"Welcome to the Hellmouth: Paradoxical Spaces in *Buffy the Vampire Slayer*" explores geographies of fear within the series through its depictions of public and private spaces. Vampires and other preternatural creatures attack the residents of Sunnydale on a daily basis. In these geographies of fear (which are largely gendered), the body is vulnerable to violence, the boundaries of homes are brutally ruptured, and streets have the possibility to become havens.

The *Fast and Furious* movie franchise frames the chapter "Home Is Where the Heart Is: *Fast and Furious* Geographies." In the series, hot bods and hot rods exist in nearly every scene, but home and family are the heart of the films. While racing in the streets drives the action of the film, a desire to reunite a constructed family and return home propels the spirit of the franchise. There are also feminist arguments to be made about how racers are treated as equals in the streets. Racing ability is more important than one's sex or gender.

The focus of "Scared to Death: Spaces of J-Horror" is horror movies. In these films, evil infiltrates private spaces including the home and the body. In these original and Westernized remakes of Japanese horror (often abbreviated J-Horror), malicious entities disturb the barriers between good and evil, interior and exterior, and living and dead. These movies often expose the porosity of the body and the home.

"Visions of Gender: Codings of Televisual Space" surveys the sites of the home and workplace in classic twentieth-century television programs. Using popular sitcoms such as *Roseanne*, *The Cosby Show*, and *Murphy Brown*, I seek to spotlight the role that television plays in forming gendered social relations of (re)production by reinforcing traditional patriarchal frameworks. The home is shown as both the masculine refuge and feminine burden, while the workplace is masculinized.

"Navigating Degrassi Community School: Socio-Spatial Identities in *Degrassi*" discusses the Canadian television series *Degrassi: The Next Generation*, which follows students at the fictitious Degrassi Community School in Toronto, Canada. The series mirrors many contemporary issues in teen life. Using the private site of the body and the public setting of the school, I focus on how reel life reflects the real situations that many teenagers in the United States and Canada face.

"Big Brother Is Watching You: Why You Should Be Watching Reality TV" investigates unscripted television. The public portrayal of private acts within these unscripted programs shows the fragility of the boundaries between the public and the private. As cameras follow participants' every move, they capture intimate acts and broadcast them via the Internet and television. The concentration is on three types of bodies portrayed in reality television: the confined body, the model body, and the body in motion. It is important to represent a diversity of bodies in television, and these programs—while promoted as "reality"—often fall short.

In "Kinky Geographies: Sexuality in Mediated Spaces," public portrayals of the body in two very different print media become the focus. Media geographies reflect and influence modern social mores regarding public and private spaces. The blog of Kitty Stryker, a sex-positive activist and writer, forms one half of the empirical example of this section and is compared to John Willie's underground fetish magazine, *Bizarre* (published 1946–59), which centered on photographs and letters from readers. Topics include bondage and discipline, domination and submission, sadism and masochism (BDSM); transvestites; extreme fashion; and other fetishes. Kitty Stryker provides a counterpoint for *Bizarre* through the sex-positive message she spreads, which can be juxtaposed with the clandestine, yet simultaneously liberating, nature of *Bizarre*. The tongue-in-cheek aspects of both case studies tie them together and develop how sexuality is explored in print spaces.

Intertextuality occurs throughout these case studies. The case studies often inform one another, as well as other media texts, and their relation to the overarching theme of public privates is examined. The common thread that links them is the notion that public and private spaces are mediated. While artificial boundaries still exist between the two spheres, there is an increased understanding of the imbrication of the two worlds. Media contribute to the breaking down of barriers between public and private. Whether the body, the home, or the street, this book seeks to understand how various media influence social constructions of these spaces and influence public and private spaces.

PUBLIC PRIVATES

1

Welcome to the Hellmouth

Paradoxical Spaces in *Buffy the Vampire Slayer*

Buffy the Vampire Slayer was my response to all the horror movies I had ever seen where some girl walks into a dark room and gets killed. So I decided to make a show where a blonde girl walks into a dark room and kicks butt instead.
—Joss Whedon

I became interested in the depiction of public and private spaces on *Buffy the Vampire Slayer* when—upon initial viewings—I noticed that there seemed to be an incredibly stark division between the two. Yet there also seemed to be contradictions in those depictions. The lead character was repeatedly shown alone and at night in what many women would typically consider to be threatening public spaces. Buffy seemed to be transgressing societal boundaries in regard to women's roles in public space, but upholding traditional roles in private.

By traditional, I mean roles that are patriarchally coded. These activities—when they differ from the expected—are deemed abnormal. *Buffy the*

Vampire Slayer follows the title character and her friends in their fight to save the world from demons and impending apocalypses in the fictional town of Sunnydale, California. I aim to offer a paradoxical reading of *Buffy the Vampire Slayer* from a feminist geographical perspective by detailing the spatial reproduction of patriarchy and resistance to it. This perspective speaks to feminist geography by arguing that it needs to consider *telespace*—spaces created by audiences watching television programs at the same time—while speaking to cultural studies of television.

The Slayer is a woman (only women are called to be Slayers) predestined to fight against evil. Along with elevated strength, the Slayer has a highly developed fighting ability and heightened intuition. As such, I argue that *Buffy the Vampire Slayer* is an illustration of a woman taking part in public space and exercising the freedom to move around within it, and, by doing so, she subverts traditional gender roles. Yet *Buffy the Vampire Slayer* also serves to reinscribe those gender roles by depicting images of violence against women in public and private spaces. Private space is also portrayed in contradictory ways. The home is shown in ways that both challenge and affirm patriarchal gender roles, both as a site of invasion/violence and as a sanctuary. These representations of private space lead to a portrait of the home as a space in which one feels safe and therefore, they adhere to reasoning that believes that women should stay in the home while, at the same time, they show the home as a site of danger which supports feminist arguments regarding domestic violence.

Sunnydale, California, the fictional setting of the *Buffy the Vampire Slayer*, is founded upon a "hellmouth"—a portal between the mystical and the earthly realms. It functions basically as a demonic mecca. Due to Sunnydale's inopportune location on this hellmouth, attacks upon Sunnydale's inhabitants (both male and female) are numerous and the mortality rate is extremely high. Buffy, with her extraordinary physical strength as a Slayer, combats the demonic forces that threaten the residents of Sunnydale.

I argue that there is both reification and destabilization of geographies of women's fear portrayed in the telespace of *Buffy the Vampire Slayer*. As Buffy claims and inhabits public space—despite very real (as opposed to imagined) threats of harm—she is providing an example of an active citizen, one who is free to move around as she pleases. The program highlights an example of an appropriation of public space within geographies of fear. Additionally, it both upholds and critiques the notion of the home as a sanctuary by discussing violence within the home, the space in which women are more likely to experience physical danger.

Media and Geographies of Fear

Buffy provides a useful example of how television informs geographical imaginations and how it can both reinforce and subvert dominant ideologies of gender and space. One's geographical imagination gets engaged when one mentally maps out the global, the regional, or the local.[1] It is basically how one conceives space. While David Harvey originated the term, the way it is used here is based on Derek Gregory's redefinition as spatialized cultural and historical interpretation.[2] Everyone has a geographical imagination—it is a way that we understand space and place.

Feminist geographers have made the link between media messages and geographical imaginations by arguing that geographical imaginations are influenced by the images and information broadcast by mass media.[3] They are concerned with how audiences—especially women—are bombarded with images of what to look like, how to act, and where to go. Media are profound and often misperceived sources of cultural pedagogy: "They contribute to educating us about how to behave and what to think, feel, believe, fear and desire—and what not to. The media are forms of pedagogy that teach us how to be men and women . . . how to react to members of different social groups . . . and how to conform to the dominant systems of norms, values, practices, and institutions."[4]

Mass media help to paint a picture in the mind's eye of what places society deems safe for women. In many cases, public space is constructed as off-limits at certain times due to threat or fear of violence, while the home is portrayed as safe. Yet these images are not monolithic, as there has been resistance. This resistance is shown by collective and individual protests (e.g., Take Back the Night) in addition to the promotion of ideas that do not conform to conventional gender norms. This issue of fear ties into feminist debates regarding the social construction of public and private spaces. For Nancy Duncan, "The public/private dichotomy (both the political and the spatial dimensions) is frequently employed to construct, control, discipline, confine, exclude, and suppress gender and sexual difference preserving traditional patriarchal and heterosexist power structures."[5] Media often help to form understandings of public and private spaces through the mental maps they cultivate.

Mental maps of fear are constructs that one uses to make daily decisions. They accumulate throughout a lifetime.[6] These maps are informed in any number of ways, but especially through everyday contact with people and the media: "Direct involvement with violence; the 'but-nothing-happened' encounters; observation of other women's degradation; the impact of the media and cultural images of women; and shared knowledge of family, friends, peers, acquaintances, and coworkers all contribute to assessment of risk and strategies for safety."[7]

Television plays a key role in forming these maps by playing on normed codings. As argued earlier, television reinforces and inscribes gender ideology onto the viewer and society. Television also helps to strengthen the hegemonic division of public and private by fortifying patriarchal geographies of fear that construct the public as dangerous and the private as safe for women: "Social critics, feminists, and academics all assert that the mass media contribute to the prevalence of fear of crime, and more specifically to female fear. They reason that the attention the media give crime and violence teaches women to fear, and continually reinforces those lessons though frequent portrayals of violence against women."[8]

Media, especially television, are important sources of information about the world around them for many people.[9] Research on the relationship between television viewing and fear of crime show that those viewers who watch programs that depict high amounts of crime have social understandings that reflect their television experience.[10] These viewers estimate crime and violence rates to be higher than they are and this leads to a cultivation of fear as well as a limitation of movement, including not walking in their neighborhoods alone at night and the complete avoidance of other neighborhoods altogether. Programs with high occurrences of violence teach viewers "to fear being a victim. Heavy viewing may lead to aggression, but for some individuals it will lead to fear and apprehension about being victimized by aggression."[11]

By promoting images of danger or harm in certain public spaces, women are discouraged from fully entering public space. These public spaces are contingent upon time of day and whether one is alone or not. Spaces that can be entered in daylight may not be ventured into at night and especially if on one's own. These places typically include those in which there are not many people about or those which are dark or dimly lit or areas that are known/perceived to have high crime rates.[12]

Buffy the Vampire Slayer portrays geographies that exemplify the mental maps or the geographical imaginations of many women. These mental maps, when based on fear, can limit the actions of women and keep them from fully participating in all aspects of public life. This fear of physical threat (although statistically more likely to happen to men) shapes the activities of women's lives.[13] Men are assaulted more frequently than women in public space, while women are assaulted more in the home. The home is not a sanctuary for some women. Many times, women limit their activities because they fear crime in the public sphere and segregate themselves in the home, yet as Gerde Wekerle and Carolyn Whitzman point out: "Despite media focus on public violence and attacks by strangers, the most dangerous place, especially for women and children, is still the home. Violence against women takes place primarily in the home, the last refuge for women increasingly fearful in most public spaces. This often results in an escalation and culmination of fear levels, as women realize that they are at risk everywhere and that no place is safe."[14] *Buffy the Vampire Slayer* helps to play into this notion as well as refute it.

Women tend to avoid certain public places because they perceive them to be dangerous or unfit for a woman.[15] Many women are careful to enact geographies of everyday life that "skirt" around areas that signify risk. These areas can range from such places as a high crime section of a city or to a neighborhood street after dark. Although these places may have few incidences of violence or harassment, their perceived image is one of threat for women. Local place mythologies are constructed based on these images transmitted through a variety of media, including news reports, movies, and television.[16]

The geography of women's fear has implications on many scales. It affects ideologies regarding the body, the home, the street, and the city. The body can become a possible site of invasion; the home can be viewed as a refuge; the street and the city become places to be feared and avoided. By avoiding public space, women restrict themselves from being full participants in public life. Fear forces women into a balancing act between public and private, between inclusion and exclusion, between fear and courage. Yet these binaries are not static and can blur and blend together to dissolve the original distinctions. Dissolution can happen by the transgression of norms within a category.

On *Buffy the Vampire Slayer*, Buffy Summers negotiates the above balancing act on a daily basis. She constantly acknowledges the tension between resistance and capitulation. *Buffy the Vampire Slayer* serves as an example of a "telespace" in and through which geographies of fear and sanctuary are constructed.[17] Sarah Radcliffe and Sallie Westwood use telespace to denote a space created by an audience watching television programs at the same time.[18] I employ this term as a useful spatial metaphor for the television-viewing community as well as a way of describing constructions of space and place within television programs.

Women are not allowed the same access to space as men because of cultural messages that dictate where they can or cannot go in order to be or to feel safe. For the majority of a woman's life, she is "groomed" as to her role in society and thus, public space. These messages are transmitted through a variety of ways. Although it is acknowledged that these messages come from many sources, including parents, teachers, and peers, messages conveyed by television are the focus of this chapter.

The Slayer and Her Watcher

The first season of *Buffy the Vampire Slayer* sets up the mythology for the series, including the legend of the aforementioned hellmouth upon which Sunnydale sits and the roles of the Slayer and the Watcher. The Slayer has two responsibilities: (1) to defeat the various demons who inhabit and congregate in Sunnydale and (2) to protect the world from imminent destruction. To aid her, the Slayer has an appointed Watcher who is designated as her mentor and trainer. The Slayer and Watcher work together as a team, with the Slayer usually performing the physical and the Watcher the mental functions of their mission. This formula becomes a bit blurred in the relationship between the Slayer Buffy and her Watcher, Giles, because he takes a more active role than most Watchers. The relationship between Buffy and her Giles is explained in more detail below.

The character of Buffy started out as a fifteen-year-old girl who was called to be the next Slayer, much to her chagrin. Buffy's strongest desire during the first season was to be "normal." To Buffy, being normal meant not having to patrol for vampires nightly, not having a sacred birthright, and not having to always wash the blood of others out of her clothing. She wanted a boyfriend, to be popular, and to be on the cheerleading squad. In the episode "Never Kill a Boy on the First Date," Buffy expresses her desire to be a typical teenage girl rather than the Slayer, a responsibility which fills her days and nights. In a conversation with her Watcher, Giles, she complains, "Clark Kent has a job. I just wanna go out on a date."[19]

Buffy's Watcher, Rupert "Ripper" Giles, plays an important function in Buffy's life as well as to the plot. He initially sought out Buffy to show her the role she would play in Sunnydale. Giles originally was the only source of knowledge regarding the preternatural until the "Scooby Gang" (consisting of Buffy, Willow, Xander, and their significant others) became research savvy.[20] Giles supervised the Sunnydale High School library, which—until its destruction in "Graduation Day, Part 2"—contained volumes and volumes of manuscripts regarding demons, demonic activities, and rites. Following graduation and obliteration of the high school, he runs the Magic Box (a store specializing in selling spell books and associated supernatural accouterments).

Giles fills a more parental role than does Buffy's mother, who through the first two seasons of the show was unaware of her daughter's status as the Slayer. Giles acts as a mentor, teacher, and surrogate father (after the Summerses divorced, Hank Summers played a virtually nonexistent role in Buffy's life) to Buffy in his role as her Watcher, in addition to training her in the ways of the supernatural. Although emotional attachments between Watchers and Slayers are not encouraged, Buffy and Giles have a caring relationship. Buffy turns to Giles in times of emotional crisis and he was the first person she called upon after discovering her mother's dead body ("The Body"). Due to the limited contact Buffy's father has with his daughter, Giles stepped in as the male authority figure for Buffy as well as her friends.

Season Synopses

The first season of *Buffy the Vampire Slayer* explores the obstacles Buffy faces in her quest to be a "normal" girl. The relationships between Buffy and those around her are the focus, especially her relationship with Angel (a vampire with a soul and her love interest) and her two best friends, Willow and Xander. Willow and Xander, along with Giles, become a support team for Buffy—a rare occurrence for a Slayer. As Spike, her archenemy in later seasons, stated, "a Slayer with family and friends. That sure as hell wasn't in the brochure" ("School Hard").

Buffy, fulfilling a prophecy, dies in a pool of water only to be revived shortly thereafter by Xander in the final episode of the first season ("Prophecy Girl"). This episode reiterates that Buffy is not in control of her own life—that she is bound by her fate—a despairing thought for a teenage girl. Buffy's death, although brief, leads to another Slayer arriving in Sunnydale in season two. For as the legend goes, once a Slayer dies, another is called.

Drusilla and Spike, two vampires from Angel's past, arrive in Sunnydale to wreak havoc upon the town in season two ("School Hard"). Angel and Buffy grow closer in their fight against Drusilla and Spike, cumulating in a sexual interlude between the two ("Innocence"). This night of passion causes Angel to lose his soul, as he has been cursed—if he experiences one moment of true happiness, then his soul will be lost. Angel reverts back to his evil former self, Angelus, and becomes Buffy's worst enemy. He terrorizes her and her friends and eventually kills Giles's girlfriend, Jenny Calendar. The killing of Ms. Calendar proved that no one was safe in Sunnydale, including major characters.

In the two-part season finale, Drusilla kills Kendra—the Slayer called when Buffy died at the end of season one—framing Buffy for the murder (although charges were later dropped). Buffy's mother finds out her secret identity as the Slayer and threatens to kick her out of the house if she continues with her slaying. Within the same episode, the principal expels Buffy from school. Just when life cannot get much worse for Buffy, Angelus finds a way to suck the world into hell. Buffy is forced to kill Angel (whose soul had been restored in a spell in the worst of timing) in order to seal the portal to hell he opened, for the only way to close the portal was with the blood that opened it.

Season three starts with Buffy living in Los Angeles attempting to start over. Her friends and family are left wondering what had become of her and if she would come back. Buffy returns to Sunnydale after realizing that her destiny as the Slayer is unavoidable and that her identity is the same regardless of location. The newest Slayer, Faith (called after Kendra's death), arrives in town shortly thereafter ("Faith, Hope, and Trick"). In the same episode that introduces Faith, Angel miraculously returns from hell and he and Buffy struggle throughout the season to keep their relationship platonic.

The arrival of Faith to Sunnydale creates a dynamic previously not seen between Buffy and another person. Although another Slayer, Kendra, had come to Sunnydale in the second season, she and Buffy did not have the same interactions as Buffy and Faith. For once in her existence in Sunnydale, Buffy was no longer the center of attention. Faith was equally as strong, equally as tough, and much more free-spirited. Faith and Buffy teamed up during the first part of season three only to become adversaries by the end as Faith's actions cause her to turn to the dark side of slaying. Season three ends with Faith comatose at the hand of Buffy, while Buffy and her Sunnydale High School classmates manage to stop the evil Mayor Wilkins's ascension on Graduation Day (although many students were killed). Angel leaves for Los Angeles after Graduation Day, leaving Buffy heartbroken.

The departure of Angel at the end of season three, as well as the destruction of Sunnydale High School, marks the end of Buffy's high school career and her move into adulthood. Buffy's plans to attend college in the fall signal that, although she accepts her Slayer duties, she has another future in mind that does not include demons. After graduation, Buffy attends the University of California–Sunnydale (UCSD) in season four and the first episodes deal with her adjustment to college life. She soon figures out that UCSD is no haven from demon activity. Buffy begins dating her psychology teaching assistant, Riley, only to find out that they both share secret lives: she as a Slayer and he as a member of a clandestine governmental organization known as the Initiative. The Initiative researches the supernatural activity in Sunnydale by capturing demons and performing experiments on them.

When the Initiative learns of Buffy's identity as a Slayer, they recruit her to join forces with them. She does so until she discovers that the head of the Initiative (her psychology professor, Dr. Walsh) wants her dead and out of the way because Buffy asks too many questions about what Buffy perceives rightly to be suspicious activities. Buffy's distrust is justified. The Initiative creates a human-demon-computer hybrid, named Adam, in order to understand the physiology of demons. Adam's programming short-circuits shortly after boot up and he plots to overthrow the human race by crafting a master race of human-demon hybrids like himself.

Buffy defeats Adam in the episode "Primeval" by combining the strengths of her friends with hers through an enjoining spell. The enjoining spell awakens the spirit of the First Slayer, who is angered by the invocation of her powers. Although Buffy wins in her battle for the lives of her friends with the First Slayer, she finds the encounter disturbing. The First Slayer (speaking through the character of Tara) warns Buffy that she is unprepared for her future: "You think you know . . . what's to come . . . what you are. You haven't even begun" ("Restless").

The fifth season of *Buffy the Vampire Slayer*, and its last on the WB network, centers on Buffy's desire to discover more about her Slayerhood and its powers after her encounter with the First Slayer. Season five introduces a new major character, Dawn, to the show. Another character—Buffy's mother, Joyce—dies. Although there was no mention of her in the first four seasons, Dawn is established as Buffy's younger sister. The explanation to this anomaly is that Dawn is "the Key" to opening all dimensions. An order of monks hid the Key in human form to protect the earth. If the Key is discovered and used, human and demon dimensions will blend into one another and chaos will ensue on earth. Glory, or the Beast, was the main villain for season five and desperately desired the Key so that she could return to her own hell dimension. The monks sent the Key to Buffy for protection and implanted in her mind memories of life with Dawn as well as those of her friends and family. Buffy and Dawn, although they eventually realize that they are not sisters in any traditional sense, love each other deeply and rely each other when Joyce first develops a brain tumor and then dies unexpectedly of an aneurysm.

The death of Joyce Summers signals another transition for Buffy. She is now responsible for her sister in a completely new way. Buffy has to play a parental role. Although still needing to take on all the Slayer duties, as in previous seasons, she has a whole new hurdle in front of her—parenting Dawn while protecting her from Glory.

Glory kidnaps Dawn despite all of Buffy's efforts and starts the ritual to open the dimensions by letting Dawn's blood. In order to close the dimensions, the blood must no longer flow. Buffy sacrifices herself as she comes to the realization that she and Dawn have the same blood. She feels that she is finally able to embrace the gift the First Slayer told her about in "Intervention"—death. Buffy plunges off a tower into the dimensional tear and prevents—once again—the end of the earth ("The Gift"). The season finale, as well as the series finale on the WB network, ends with a shot of Buffy's tombstone, which reads: "Buffy Anne Summers, 1981–2000, Beloved Sister, Devoted Friend, She Saved the World a Lot."

The series moved networks for its sixth season. After Buffy's death, Giles returns to England while Willow and Xander hatch a plan to resurrect Buffy as they believe she may have been sent to hell. Their beliefs were wrong (Buffy was actually in heaven) and the story arc for the season mostly focuses on Buffy's grief at being resurrected from heaven. In her grief-stricken state, Buffy begins a sexual relationship with Spike, her former enemy. The relationship turns sour after Spike attempts to rape her. She also battles the villains of the season—the Trio—who accidentally kill Tara (Willow's girlfriend) while trying to kill Buffy. Willow becomes enmeshed in dark magic following Tara's death and exacts revenge on the Trio, killing Warren (the leader of the Trio) by skinning him alive. Willow eventually succumbs to the dark magic and tries to end her suffering by destroying the world. Xander offers her unconditional love, which fends off the apocalypse.

The seventh and final season focuses on the First Evil and Buffy's attempts to vanquish it. Sunnydale High School has been reconstructed and Buffy secures a job there. The only issue: the school still sits on the hellmouth. Spike has his soul restored as atonement for his actions toward Buffy and lives in the basement of the school, now driven insane by the First Evil.

Potential Slayers gather in Sunnydale after the Watchers' Council is destroyed. The lives of the Potential Slayers are in danger and seek protection under Buffy and Giles, who has returned from England. The First Evil proves too much for Buffy to handle on her own, even with the assistance of her friends and the Potentials. The First Evil amasses a legion of primitive vampires (Turok-Han), who are more powerful than the human-demon hybrid Buffy is accustomed to fighting. Buffy and Faith, who has come back to Sunnydale, reunite to fight together as Slayers against the First Evil.

In the series finale, Buffy returns to the hellmouth where it all started to fight the Turok-Han and the First Evil. Angel returns to give Buffy an amulet that will help her and to fight alongside her. Initially lopsided, the fight evens out when Willow invokes a spell that activates the transformation of the Potentials into Slayers. With their new powers, they hold back the army of Turok-Han long enough for the amulet the reformed Spike has been given to activate. The amulet explodes, destroying both the hellmouth and Spike. Sunnydale collapses into a crater, and thus ends the show.

Representations of Public Space

This section discusses both the sanctioning and the support of subversive behavior in public space in *Buffy the Vampire Slayer* and deals, more specifically, with representations of women in public space and the implications these have on formulations of gendered geographies of fear. Representations of public space on television can help to reinforce societal norms of proper behavior in public space. If inappropriate action is taken, then sanctions can be shown to uphold traditional ideology. Conversely, when action deemed socially inappropriate is taken and no punishments are portrayed, then a crack could be formed in the hegemonic framework.

Sunnydale is a magnet for demons. The city has extremely high rates of violence due to the presence of these otherworldly entities, and no place is safe from the threat of violence. Typically, "vampires generally lurk in the 'bad places'—cemeteries, dark alleys, basements and tunnels, abandoned buildings, and suburban parks. [Yet] in Sunnydale . . . they also lurk in the ordinary spaces where contemporary teens are exposed to urban threats: dance clubs, high school locker rooms, classrooms, lounges, and parking lots, shopping malls, and private homes."[21]

At Sunnydale High School and the University of California–Sunnydale, deaths are a common occurrence as they are everywhere in Sunnydale. For example, the high school yearbook had an "In Memoriam" section that included over twenty names in one year. Parent-Teacher Night was inundated with vampires ("School Hard"). Class is cancelled due to a "dead body in a locker" ("Welcome to the Hellmouth"). Werewolves attack students crossing campus ("Beauty and the Beasts"). Dormitory roommates turn out to be soul-stealing demons that strike when you sleep ("Living Conditions"). The town lives in a state of denial regarding its hellmouth status. Demons are never to blame; instead the disappearances and attacks are attributed to such things as gangs on drugs or wild dogs. At the local all-ages hangout, the Bronze, vampires and other demons are ubiquitous. It has even been referred to as "a breeding ground for vampire activity" within the show ("Welcome to the Hellmouth"). Unsuspecting patrons are lured into the dark recesses of the club by vampires, drank from, and left to die. A passionate embrace in a corner may not be exactly as it seems. Vampires, trolls, angry gods, and others attack local shops frequently. One can only imagine the lost revenue due to preternatural activity and wonder if insurance policies covering acts of God include any god.

Sunnydale represents an example of extreme geographies of women's fear. I acknowledge that *Buffy the Vampire Slayer* is a television program with a fantastic premise that requires suspension of disbelief. Yet the premise of the program should not be a distraction, but can instead be used as a tool to examine the socio-spatial dialectic within representations of public and private spaces. The spaces portrayed within the show take on saliency as they become incorporated into the viewer's geographical imagination. It is the very fact that vampires inhabit Sunnydale that makes the title character's actions so important. Buffy's actions are significant because she occupies public space in the face of such overwhelming danger.

The attacks upon Sunnydale's inhabitants are not usually from strangers, but from friends, classmates, lovers, and the like. Joss Whedon, the creator of the *Buffy the Vampire Slayer* program, discusses one of the practical aspects of this within the show: "For example, vampires look like vampires part of the time, because I want to see demons so you don't have a high school girl just stabbing people. At the same time, I want her to see people that [the viewer] doesn't know if they're vampires or not."[22]

Since the demon retains the human form, an uncertainty is created as to who poses a threat. The show debunks the myth of the stranger as danger, thereby destabilizing the notion that it is the public, the unknown, which is to be feared. In Sunnydale, both the familiar and the strange can be potential sources or sites of danger.

Public Space as Dangerous

Many times Buffy encounters vampires attacking patrons in the alley outside of the Bronze, the local hangout. Inside—within the darkly lit setting—the club is equally as dangerous. Buffy has rescued many patrons from an untimely demise both inside and outside the Bronze. The Bronze typifies what Buffy battles against each night, but I would also like to highlight and discuss places in Sunnydale other than the Bronze or the numerous cemeteries that Buffy patrols and is attacked in nightly. By doing so, I show how places more familiar to the viewer's everyday life are coded.

The following scene from the episode "Phases" highlights the dangers of walking alone at night in Sunnydale. Theresa, one of Buffy's class-mates, is traveling home. The night is dark and no streetlights are visible. Nobody is seen on the sidewalk except for Theresa. The houses that she passes are not lit. Theresa is surrounded by nothing but manicured lawns and darkness. As she is walking, she hears noises. Suspicious, she looks around and sees nothing. Theresa begins to walk, but the rustling of leaves continues. She once more stops to survey the situation. After hearing a growl, she begins to run. Looking behind her, she collides with Angelus and screams upon impact. Angelus asks her if everything is fine and Teresa explains the reason for her anxiety to him. He assuages her fears by reassuring her that there is no one out there and states, "It can get pretty scary out here, all alone at night." Seeing that she is still nervous, Angelus mentions that he recognizes her as a classmate of Buffy's and offers to walk her home. Relaxing, she agrees and they head off together. Little does Theresa know that her trusted companion will soon kill her and make her a vampire like himself.

This scene is a televisual example of a woman carefully navigating her walk home through public space. As Theresa is alone and it is dark, she is very conscious of the noises she hears. When she becomes very afraid, she begins to run to lessen her time in the threatening space. Unfortunately for her, her fear is well founded and the consequences of her actions are fatal. This episode reinforces the representation of public space as dangerous for women and helps to promote the mental map of fear by showing images of a woman justifiably fearful in public space.

In the episode "Checkpoint," Buffy is taking a shortcut through a dark alley, late for an evening appointment with Giles and the Watchers' Council. She picks up her pace after checking her watch and is suddenly tackled from behind. Buffy and her attacker stand up and face off. They fight briefly, until two more attackers appear. She is encircled threateningly and the scene cuts to a commercial. This scene shows again how walking alone at night as a woman can cause bodily harm. Buffy takes a shortcut to save time, but the added time she saves is traded for the "protection" of the main thoroughfare and its streetlights.

Similar to both of the above episodes, "Hush" also portrays scenes that involve the assault of a woman walking alone at night in an isolated, unpopulated, dimly lit public space. This time the character of Tara is the one targeted. Tara is walking home alone from the library with a stack of books in hand. She is on the UCSD campus, yet no other students are around. There is little light, barring moonlight. The shrubbery, which defines the pathway on which she walks, is dense. As she moves, the only sounds to be heard initially are the soft sounds of her footsteps. On her way back to her dorm room, Tara finds herself in the familiar situation of being alone at night and hearing noises. As she looks behind her, she falls over some shrubbery, losing the books she was holding in the process. As she gathers her belongings, four attackers can be seen approaching in the background. The men following her are "the Gentlemen" and their henchmen who have come to Sunnydale to steal the hearts of seven residents in order to fulfill a prophecy. Tara hears the men approaching and looks up. Seeing them, she begins to run and is consequently chased through campus.

In "Halloween," Buffy is transformed by a magical spell into her costume as are the other patrons of Ethan's Costume Shop. Those who are dressed as monsters, vampires, werewolves, devils, and the like literally become them and run amuck throughout Sunnydale. Unfortunately for the residents of Sunnydale, Buffy's costume of choice is that of an eighteenth-century noblewoman. Buffy chose that particular costume in an attempt to please her boyfriend, Angel, thinking that he preferred the demure women of his mortal time to the more aggressive women of the present. On the one night that undead activity is typically low, the streets of Sunnydale are overrun with monsters and people fleeing to find shelter. Miniature witches, goblins, and vampires wreak havoc upon Sunnydale. Sidewalks are teeming with mischievous activity. Parked cars are vandalized; storefront windows are broken. Those not under the curse's effects run for their lives, seeking refuge within their cars or homes.

As a result of the curse, Buffy forgets that she is a Slayer and becomes unable to look after or defend herself in the face of danger. After a vampire enters her house, Buffy flees to the streets of Sunnydale, running blindly with fright. Seeing the chaos on the main streets, she becomes more frightened and—in seeking to avoid the melee—she finds herself in a dark alley. The alley is dark and cramped, filled with dumpsters and crates. Ever darker shadows mask the nooks and crannies created by the clutter. Looking around, she decides what course of action to take next. She lifts her skirt a bit and starts to walk. She turns around to look behind her only to find that a pirate has closed in on her. He leers at her and then begins to give chase as she runs away. Buffy trips over her long gown and the pirate pins her up against a crate. As the pirate moves in to kiss her, Xander—who has become a soldier for the evening—rescues her.

These scenes are images that contribute to geographies of women's fear in which public space is constructed as hazardous and as a site of potential assault. The repetition of these scenarios of women walking alone at night is drilled into the viewer's head as a dangerous activity. They reinforce and construct a patriarchal ideology that frames the mental maps of women. Through these media representations, women learn to fear public space and to view it as a site of danger in certain situations. Their movements in public space become limited and reflect the ideologies that teach them to restrict their actions.

It is not only outdoor public space in which danger occurs. Sunnydale High School was the site of several attacks upon students and faculty. In the following scene from "Passion," Angelus surprises Jenny Calendar in her classroom late one night. Jenny has been working on a soul restoration spell to convert Angelus back to Angel and has finally succeeded. While she is printing out a hardcopy of the spell, Jenny realizes that Angelus is in the classroom with her. Only the glow from the computer monitor lights the empty room. The students' desks are shadowed and the recesses of the room are black. Terrified, Jenny rises from her desk inching toward the door and asks Angelus how he entered the building. Angelus replies, "I was invited. The sign in front of the school . . . 'Formatia trans sicere educatorum'" (Enter all ye who seek knowledge). Angelus lunges towards Jenny and she begins to run. After a struggle, Jenny breaks free and scrambles out into the hallway.

The hallway, like the classroom, is dark and empty. The doors to the classrooms and offices are shut and the lockers provide no possibility of protection. Angelus chases her throughout the school, "working up an appetite." The chase scene is quite detailed and extended. After being hunted for several minutes, Jenny thinks she has finally lost Angelus. She runs up the stairs only to be met by him. Although the rest of the school is dark, a window at the top of the stairs bathes the pair in moonlight. Angelus holds Jenny close and breaks her neck, whispering, "This is where you get off."

In "School Hard," vampire Spike and his cronies overtake the Parent-Teacher Night at Sunnydale High School. As parents, teachers, and students nervously mill about the sterile teacher's lounge bringing the evening to a close, two vampires suddenly come crashing into the lounge, overturning tables and chairs, and scattering refreshments on the floor. Several more vampires follow the initial two and soon the room is taken over. Everyone begins to panic as the vampires line up. Buffy and her mother eventually make it out of the lounge after Buffy throws a chair at Spike, distracting him. The vampires barricade all exits to the school, making it inescapable. The power is shut off to the school and the vampires have the school surrounded. Spike grabs a man and kills him for the fun of it by breaking his neck saying, "You're too old to eat. But not to kill. I feel better."

In the episode "Prophecy Girl," a roomful of bodies is discovered by Willow. The students have been killed as part of the impending apocalypse prophesied to beset the world unless Buffy defeats the Master, a powerful vampire who has been trapped in a dimensional portal for centuries. Willow enters the audiovisual room at Sunnydale High and finds the dead bodies of her classmates. The room is completely disheveled and there is a bloody handprint on one of the television screens. Later in the episode, Willow describes her feelings to Buffy: "I'm not okay. I knew those guys. I go to that room every day. And when I walked in there, it . . . it wasn't our world anymore. They made it theirs."

Another school slaying happens in the episode "Becoming, Part 1." Kendra, the Slayer called when Buffy temporarily died at the end of season one, is alone in the school library with Drusilla, a vampire who is in cahoots with Angelus to destroy the world. Drusilla hypnotizes Kendra and slashes Kendra's throat while she is under her spell. Drusilla whispers, "night-night" and kisses the air.

The scenes described here contribute to the reinforcement of a hegemonic ideology, which teaches women that they should not be alone in public space at night. The school is a site of fear in these scenes. It is not only the dark streets and alleyways that are to be avoided, but all unpopulated and dark public spaces. The message is that being alone in public places after dark is dangerous and life threatening. It reinscribes upon the geographical imagination areas to be avoided because of threat of danger. Each of these scenes shows the implications of transgressing the public-private divide.

Appropriation of Public Space

As the Slayer, Buffy is afforded an opportunity that many women are not. She is able to walk freely through space and feels confident in her ability to do so due to her heightened abilities. This is not to say that she is without fear, but she does not let her fear hamper her mobility or restrict her from public space. By occupying and taking action in public space, Buffy is challenging the social order that seeks to exclude her in order to "protect" her. Contrary to needing protection, it is Buffy who does the guarding of her fellow Sunnydale citizens. In her senior year in high school, Buffy was named as "Class Protector" since many of her fellow students had become aware of her status as a Slayer ("The Prom"). This shows an example of a woman doing the protecting, instead of needing to be protected. She takes an active, instead of passive, role in her actions. If there is a threat, she will seek it out and neutralize it.

Within the numerous cemeteries of Sunnydale, Buffy patrols at night actively searching for demons. She is attacked frequently, yet these attacks are expected. Buffy does not let her fear stop her. She seeks out and resists the hegemonic spatial coding. Although Buffy uses her stake, "Mr. Pointy," as a protective device similar to that of Mace or pepper spray, she uses that device as a means to access and appropriate space. Almost every episode opens with a fight sequence between Buffy and one or more vampires. Typically, the setting is one of the many Sunnydale cemeteries. She is usually patrolling alone at night when the attack occurs. Sometimes the vampires rise up out of their graves behind her or lurk behind large headstones or mausoleums. Sometimes the fight is completely one-sided in Buffy's favor, other times it is a more equal battle, but Buffy always prevails. Shortly before she stakes the vampires, she delivers a witty pun just to punctuate her authority.

Many episodes provide examples of Buffy in an active role in public space or as that of a protector of her fellow Sunnydale residents. After being surrounded by her attackers in "Checkpoint," for example, Buffy begins to fight with them. One of the men swings at Buffy with a sword, but she is able to hold him off as well as the other two men coming at her with staffs. Kicking, spinning, and punching, she is able to defend herself against three assailants. After thoroughly pummeling all three, she sends them on their way after finding out why they attacked her.

In the episode "Halloween," Spike catches up to Buffy who is still assuming the identity of an eighteenth-century noblewoman after Xander takes care of Buffy's first attacker of the night, the pirate. Spike has Buffy backed up against a crate and slaps her, obviously enjoying himself. The spell is broken just as Spike prepares to bite Buffy. Spike tugs at Buffy's hair to bring her to standing only to find that he has only a wig in his hands. Surprised, he looks at her only to realize that her Slayer powers are back. Buffy then punches and kicks Spike as they battle in a warehouse. They spar with lead pipes and Buffy is able to bring him down swiftly with an uppercut to the chin. Stunned and shaken, Spike gets up and quickly retreats.

Threat comes in a different form in the episode "Shadow." As the Scooby Gang is nestled in at the local magic shop one evening, they are interrupted by a giant serpent that has been sent by Glory to seek out the Key. The serpent can barely fit the width of its body within the magic shop door and towers over the group. Suddenly afraid, the snake leaves and Buffy pursues the monstrous creature. The snake slithers violently down the weakly lit street, moving cars and pedestrians out of its path. Buffy continues to chase the snake throughout the streets of Sunnydale until she catches up with it in a wooded area. The wooded area borders a park, but is dark and desolate. Jumping up onto a large rock, Buffy attempts to strangle the serpent with a piece of chain she has picked up in her pursuit. Unable to strangle him effectively, she wrestles and punches the serpent until she defeats it and it lies motionless. In this episode, Buffy once again serves as protector both of her sister and of the citizens of Sunnydale whose lives the snake was threatening. Unafraid and determined, Buffy followed the snake all through Sunnydale in order to slay it.

In another instance of protecting Sunnydale's residents, Buffy is finally able to take revenge upon the Gentlemen late in the episode "Hush." As she is out patrolling to keep order in the silent, but chaotic, city, Buffy spies the Gentlemen's lackeys. As she flips one to the ground, another grabs her from behind. She grapples with the henchmen and brings them down. Buffy then notices that another minion has headed into the clock tower and she gives chase. Inside the clock tower, Buffy is surprised to run into Riley, her psychology teaching assistant and boyfriend, but does not allow the shock to faze her. After subduing the lackeys, Buffy notices a box sitting on a table similar to one she had had a prophetic dream about earlier in the episode. Realizing that it holds the voices of the citizens of Sunnydale, she smashes it open. Recovering her own voice, Buffy destroys the Gentlemen by screaming. The sound of Buffy's scream causes the Gentlemen's heads to burst. This episode highlights another example of Buffy taking action when others would not. She patrolled the streets of Sunnydale to make sure that panic did not envelope the residents and was able to cure the mysterious "laryngitis" that had overtaken the town (as it was explained by the evening news).

Although prophesied to die if she faces the Master, Buffy still takes him on in "Prophecy Girl." Buffy must die in order for the Master to ascend from the dimension in which he is trapped, and it is foretold that she will. She enters the Master's lair in order to fulfill her destiny. The Master's lair is a former church, lit solely by candles. Dead and rotting bodies lie about the sunken and decaying building. After drinking her blood, the Master drops Buffy in a shallow pool of water causing her to drown. Xander—who has followed Buffy in order to prevent her from facing the Master—resuscitates her. Shortly after Xander performs CPR and brings her back, the tenacious Buffy heads to the center of the hellmouth to finish her fight with the Master. She finds him and throws him through a skylight, impaling him, and causing his body to turn to ash. Although the hellmouth portal had temporarily opened, the demise of the Master seals it. Buffy staves off another apocalypse. This episode is a particularly illuminating example of the courage that Buffy shows in the face of danger. She knew she was going to die, yet she still did not let her fear hamper what needed to be done.

I would argue that *Buffy the Vampire Slayer* can be viewed as an attempt to reverse the hegemonic discourse of fear for women in public. I have highlighted the potential subversion and/or destabilization of patriarchal codings of space in *Buffy the Vampire Slayer* in order to show how public space is constructed and gendered, sometimes paradoxically so. Public space is represented as threatening and dangerous, yet Buffy frequently appropriates that space and thereby undermines hegemonic ideologies regarding women and public space.

Buffy is active in public space under threatening conditions. She subverts the dominant representation of gendered geographies of fear by seeking out and occupying public spaces that are constructed as threatening or dangerous. According to Linda McDowell, "Feminist campaigns to 'appropriate the streets' or 'appropriate the night,' along with counterclaims for curfews for men, challenge the assumed greater freedom for men to occupy open and public space."[23] These attempts to "take back the night" show an active, not a passive, use of space and acceptance of social order. As Hille Koskela argues: "Women are not merely objects in space where they experience restrictions and obligations; they also actively produce, define, and appropriate space."[24]

Representations of Private Space

Representations of private spaces in *Buffy the Vampire Slayer* are depicted paradoxically in two ways: as sanctuaries and as sites of invasion. There are repercussions of these portrayals for the formation of mental maps and gendered geographies of fear for both men and women. The representation of the home as a sanctuary or refuge plays into patriarchal codings of space in which the private is seen as safe, as opposed to the dangerous public. The home as a site of invasion helps to support feminist theories regarding domestic violence and statistics that show that women are more likely to be attacked within their own homes.

Home as Sanctuary

In *Buffy the Vampire Slayer*, there are few instances in which private space is portrayed as safe. They mostly occur when a vampire shows up on the doorstep and is unable to enter due to the necessity for an invitation. Two scenes from the show provide examples of the fortification of the home, where those who were once invited are now not.

In the first scene, upon discovering that Angelus has entered Willow's house as well as hers without their knowledge, Buffy asks Giles to find a spell to "de-invite" Angelus from their homes in the episode "Passion." Angelus intercepts Joyce one night as she gets out of her Jeep Cherokee after grocery shopping and walks with her up to the doorway of the Summerses' home. Standing on the lawn in front of the brightly lit two-story ranch-style home, Angelus attempts to explain to Joyce that he is having difficulty sleeping since the night that he and Buffy made love and that he needs to talk to Buffy. Joyce, visibly distraught, fumbles with her keys and unlocks the front door. Angelus tries to enter, but an invisible barrier impedes him. Surprised, he looks up to see Buffy and Willow coming down the stairs. Buffy leads while Willow reads a Latin verse from a book, "Hicce verbis consensus rescissus est," which translates to "By these strong unanimous words [Angelus' permission to enter] is rescinded." Buffy approaches the doorway, states that the locks have been changed, and slams the door in his face.

By revoking Angelus's power to enter the house, Buffy has created a sanctuary for her family and friends as well as herself. Although the home is typically off-limits to a vampire, Buffy had removed that barrier by inviting Angel into the Summerses' home in a previous episode ("Angel"). With the reinstating of the barricade, Buffy has effectively reinforced the notion that the private is a haven and a site of protection.

In a situation similar to that in "Passion," in another scene Buffy once again needs to withdraw permission for a vampire to enter. After Spike has revealed his love for her (while threatening to kill her if she does not return it) Buffy implements the spell again. Spike follows Buffy home one night. As Buffy approaches her home, she opens the door and enters. Spike, directly behind her, states, "Like it or not, I'm in your life; you can't just shut me out." He tries to follow Buffy into the house, but is unable. Spike stares at the doorway in surprise, unsure as to what has happened. Once Spike realizes that his invitation to the Summerses' home has been repealed, Buffy closes the door.

These scenes help to reinforce the image of the home as a sanctuary and a place within which to take refuge from the dangerous public sphere. The ability to rescind the invitation to enter a house can be seen a way of controlling domestic space and asserting a claim over it. The following section seeks to show the link between the home and violence and to deflate the myth of the home as invariably a haven.

Invasion of Home

The episode "Passion" opens with Angelus stalking Buffy and her friends outside of a club and then following her home. He watches Buffy as she walks along arm in arm, joking with her friends. As she nestles into bed, Angelus watches through the window. The night wears on and Buffy lies sleeping in her bed, snuggled in her pink-and-white comforter and sheets. Angelus sits on the edge of her bed, stroking her hair while she sleeps. When she wakes in the morning, Buffy finds a charcoal drawing that Angelus has done during the night, proof that he has been inside her room and she was unable to protect herself, her family, or her home against the invasion.

Not only did Angelus infiltrate her home, he invaded the private within the private. He has occupied one of her most intimate and secure spaces, her sleep. Buffy is completely unaware of the incursion and is relaxed, not knowing that danger is imminent.

Later in the same episode, Willow is in her bedroom feeding her fish while she and Buffy talk on the phone. Willow is standing in her pajamas in front of the tank, the camera shooting her through the water in the aquarium. They are discussing the situation of Angelus when Willow suddenly notices an envelope on her bed. Willow is disconcertingly silent and Buffy demands a reply from her. Willow looks again at her aquarium and notices there are no fish. Opening the envelope, she pulls out a string upon which her fish are hung. Willow drops the phone in shock and ends up spending the night at Buffy's house, unwilling to be in hers, perceiving it as a site of invasion.

Buffy and Willow are violated within their most private spaces as young women, their bedrooms. As teenagers, they spend a lot of time in their rooms discussing subjects they do not want their parents to overhear. Angelus violated their sanctuary from the adult world. Additionally, Buffy and Willow are portrayed in moments of stereotypically feminine behavior or settings. Buffy is nestled in a bed decorated in pastel colors and when Willow finds her fish in the envelope, she is engaged in a telephone conversation with Buffy, a nightly ritual for many teenage girls. These moments can be interpreted as showing the vulnerable female, but the next scene discussed shows that it is not only the female characters who experience invasion.

After killing Jenny at Sunnydale High School, Angelus moves her body to Giles's apartment to torment him further. Giles arrives home later that evening to find a red rose on the door and can hear music playing inside. Thinking a romantic evening is in store for Jenny and himself, he steps inside with a smile. Seeing a note on the table that directs him upstairs, he climbs the stairs with champagne in hand. The stairs are strewn with rose petals and there is a candle on each step to light his way. When he reaches the top of the stairs, he sees Jenny lying lifeless on his bed. Next to her is a charcoal drawing that Angelus left behind as his calling card.

Private space is invaded once again in "Hush." After hearing a knock on the door to his college dorm room late one night, a young man awakens and opens the door. Standing in a dark room, he is momentarily blinded by the bright light in the hallway. He is grabbed by the men at the door and held down on his bed. Unable to scream due to a spell put on the town removing everyone's voices, he is cut open by the Gentlemen and his heart removed.

These scenes show how various predators and threats can invade the home. These invasions of private space show that the home is not always a sanctuary, but can also be a place of fear. This supports feminist arguments regarding domestic violence, while at the same time contributes to a destabilization of the notion that only the public space is to be avoided based on fear of danger.

The episode "Ted" once again subverts the notion of the home as sanctuary, but in this episode the threat takes on a more "familiar" form—that of a potential step-father. Buffy's mother, Joyce, has begun to date a man who seems idyllic to the outside world, yet Buffy is apprehensive of him. As the episode progresses, there are several instances in which Ted threatens Buffy. In one, Ted catches Buffy cheating at miniature golf and he informs her that he won't stand for that sort of "malarkey" in his house, while pounding his golf club repeatedly. When Buffy retorts that it's a good thing they're not *in* his house, Ted replies, "Do you want me to smack that smart-ass mouth of yours?" Later in the episode, Buffy returns home to find Ted in her room, riffling through her things and reading her journal. Buffy tries to take her diary back and Ted punches her. Buffy and Ted fight until he falls down the stairs and lies motionless. Joyce looks on in horror and accuses Buffy of killing him. The police arrive on the scene and declare it a case of self-defense.

Joyce sends Buffy to her room (apparently the punishment for homicide—albeit in self-defense—is a time-out). Frustrated by her situation, Buffy tries to sneak out through her window but it is nailed shut. Suddenly, Ted appears in her room behind her. He grabs Buffy around the throat and pins her against a wall. In retaliation she stabs him with a nail file only to reveal that his arm is full of wires and that Ted is a robot.

Ted eventually knocks Buffy out, then heads downstairs to see Joyce. He informs Joyce that he was dead for six minutes but then revived. Ted tries to get Joyce to leave with him, but his stutter (an electronic malfunction caused by the stabbing) makes her cautious. Aggravated, Ted hits Joyce and knocks her unconscious. He hears Buffy moving around and attempts to hunt her down, but Buffy hits him with an iron skillet, tearing the skin off his face to reveal his robotic skull and deactivating him for good.

The interaction between Ted and Buffy highlights another invasion of the home. Not only does Ted assault Buffy and Joyce within their home, he tries to infiltrate their family. Buffy's reluctance to accept Ted into her familial life shows us another instance of where her Slayer intuition has paid off and she is able to protect her family again.

Private space in *Buffy the Vampire Slayer* is represented as both a haven and a place of assault. These contradictory portrayals contribute to both the strengthening and undermining of hegemonic narratives of private space. By showing the home as a refuge, a patriarchal coding of private space is reinforced by juxtaposing the public the sphere as dangerous. Representations that depict the private as a sanctuary reiterate the ideology that one should avoid public space as it is perceived to be dangerous and threatening. The home as a site of invasion helps to counter these hegemonic notions of public and private space by showing that it is not only public space that is a space of fear. Combined with those of public space, the representations of private space in *Buffy the Vampire Slayer* create a paradoxical depiction of geographies of fear.

Femininity/Musculinity

Buffy was created to "look the part of the blonde bimbo who dies in reel two, but turns out to be anything but that."[25] The type of femininity that Buffy exhibits can be viewed in multiple ways. To some viewers, Buffy could be seen as contributing to standard notions of femininity by being very conscious of her looks. The physical stereotype of beauty that the character represents (white, blond, tan, and slender) could be viewed as promoting an idealized image of beauty—similar to that of Barbie—which most women cannot attain. Therein lies the irony. She is a former Valley Girl who has a sacred birthright. She wears leather pants and feathered, fringed halter tops to slay demons. The character is sexed, raced, and classed in such a way as to not be transgressive in any way other than by her actions. Buffy's physical appearance can be analyzed in ways ranging from catering to hegemonic standards of beauty to an ironic framework that situates Buffy as looking like the damsel in distress, but playing the heroine instead. This irony lends itself to a more subversive reading of the show.

I argue that the character's style of femininity could also be interpreted and read with a feminist lens as well as with as being read as a specimen of patriarchal expectations and notions of femininity. She can serve an example of a female action protagonist that is not overtly masculinized or "musculinized": "The masculinsation of the female body, which is effected most visibly through muscles, can be understood in terms of a notion of 'musculinity.' That is, some of the qualities associated with masculinity are written over the muscular female body. Musculinity indicates the way in which signifiers of strength are not limited to male characters."[26] Buffy counters the female "action figure" stereotype through her physical attributes. She is not bulked up and muscular like many of her predecessor in the action genre (think of the character of Sarah Connor in the *Terminator* series, Ripley in the *Aliens* franchise, or see my later discussion of the *Fast and Furious* films), but is instead quite petite. She is, however, supernaturally strong.

The character of Buffy Summers both undermines and reproduces hegemonic notions of femininity. When the show first started, Buffy was a fifteen-year-old girl obsessed with the perfect date outfit, bouncy hair, and the color of her nail polish. Over the run of the series, while her priorities have changed from dating to running a household, she still has a keen eye for fashion. Typically clad in halter tops or tank tops and short skirts, Buffy exemplifies the stereotype of a "girly-girl." With such stereotypical depictions of femininity, Buffy helps to reproduce patriarchal constructions of beauty. Julie D'Acci argues that "TV depictions . . . may have a very real correlation to our conceptions of what 'woman' (as a notion produced in language and discourse) and 'women' (as historical human beings) are and can be. They may take an active part in fashioning our social, sexual, and gendered possibilities and positions, as well as our behaviors and our very bodies."[27]

Yet Buffy also counteracts stereotypical notions of how "women" should be. Although she may look like a model, her actions do not exactly fit the mold of how most women are represented in media. Buffy subverts ideas of patriarchal gender roles by her role as aggressor. Shirley Ardener discusses how the horror genre can permit more fluidity in representations of masculinity and femininity: "The vulnerability of women is made much of in fiction; indeed, most horror movies rely upon viewers imagining women being violated, while they sometimes also provide for the woman's ultimate rescue from attack, making this more socially acceptable. Such fiction (that involving vampires, for example) may at the same time have a mythic quality and perhaps belongs to the world-wide genre in which social norms are reversed."[28]

Buffy the Vampire Slayer provides an example of a representation in which a woman reverses norms, yet this is limited in its counter-hegemonic effect as it is depicted as part of a myth and not as reality. As Susan Owen discusses: "Buffy's embodied strength, power, and assertiveness destabilize the traditional masculinist power of the vampire character in the horror genre, in effect policing those who prey upon the feminized. The series gleefully transposes conventional relations of power between the body-that-bleeds and the bloodsuckers."[29] A possibility also exists for a destabilization of gendered geographies of fear by "restaging the relationship between women and violence as not only one of danger in which women are objects of violence but also a pleasurable one in which women retaliate to become the agents of violence and turn the table on their aggressors."[30]

Blurring of Boundaries, Dissolution of Binaries

Horror can be used in a way to show the social and cultural constructions of space. As Ken Gelder argues, "Horror can sometimes find itself championed as a genre because the disturbance it willfully produces is in fact a disturbance of cultural and ideological categories we may have taken for granted."[31] These disturbances can create "public privates" through the blurring of spatial boundaries.

Buffy the Vampire Slayer also blurs time and space through the use of multiple time and space dimensions within the show ("The Wish, "Doppelgangland," "Beauty and the Beasts," "Anne"). These include parallel realities in which vampires rule the earth and a bevy of hells (both Angel and Buffy have entered alternate dimensions). While the parallel realities have a similar time scale, time is elongated within hells; while a relatively short amount of time has passed in Sunnydale, eons will have elapsed in hell. With these notions of space and time, *Buffy the Vampire Slayer* allows for a more fluid spatiality. The production of space becomes even more apparent as multiple possibilities of spatialities are portrayed. For instance, one episode focuses on what Sunnydale would be like without Buffy ("The Wish") and another on Sunnydale overrun by a vampiric Willow and Xander ("Doppelgangland"). Yet these episodes are not merely "what if" scenarios. Within the framework of the show, these events really did happen and are a part of the character's memories. Buffy's sister, Dawn, is a perfect example of a created, constructed entity. Dawn originally was just energy until she was transformed into a human being by an order of monks. Memories of her false birth and her life were remembered not only by Dawn, but by everyone connected to Buffy's life, whether they were in Sunnydale, Los Angeles, or London.

Additionally, time becomes less of a constraint when dealing with immortal beings such as vampires. Time within *Buffy the Vampire Slayer* is not bounded by the human life span, but instead is eternal. They are able to experience changes that occur over centuries. The viewer is permitted to see history as the characters have lived it.

Vampiric Geographies

Vampires also can be used symbolically. Vampires have been used as metaphors for topics ranging from capitalism to colonialism to homophobia.[32] The use of metaphor is important because "metaphors offer us insights not simply into linguistics or rhetoric, but a culture itself."[33] As times change, so do vampires. Nina Auerbach posits that "every age embraces the vampire it needs."[34] As such, the vampire can represent the fears of a society for itself. Joan Gordon and Veronica Hollinger state that "myths and legends surrounding the vampire do not describe an actual physical being, but something much more powerful, a creature who can take on the allegorical weight of changing times and collective psyches."[35]

The vampire is an example of a pharmakon, that which is neither and both. Jacques Derrida defines the pharmakon as both remedy and poison.[36] Pharmakons provide a "both-ness" and a "between-ness" as do vampires. They are both human and demon and exist between the mortal realm and the immortal. The pharmakon sets up and disrupts binaries simultaneously because it is both ends of the binary at the same time. It is both and either.

Isabel Pinedo shows how the vampire does this: "The pallor of the vampire, the weirdly oxymoronic "living dead" signifies death, yet the sated vampire's veins surge with the blood of its victim. The monster disrupts the social order by dissolving the basis of its signifying system, its network of differences: me/not me, animate/inanimate, human/nonhuman, life/death. The monster's body dissolves binary differences."[37] In one of the most famous texts regarding vampires, *Dracula*, Van Helsing interprets Dracula as both "a primitive throwback and a Nietzschean harbinger of an advanced, inhuman race."[38] The vampire is a hybrid of extremes.

Apprehension is created within the viewing audience as it is unknown whether the person confronted is friend or foe. The vampire strikes a chord of terror within us because "it is the monster that used to be human; it is the undead that used to be alive; it is the monster that *looks like us*. For this reason, the figure of the vampire always has the potential to jeopardize conventional distinctions between human and monster, between life and death, between ourselves and the other."[39]

The attacks upon Sunnydale's inhabitants are not usually from strangers, but from friends, classmates, lovers, and so on. Since the demon retains the human form, an uncertainty is created. Additionally, this leads to the debunking of the myth of the stranger as danger within the show.

Private space is still represented as a refuge from outside danger prevalent in the public space. In the streets of Sunnydale, public space is dangerous space. Dark alleys become sites of attack and even murder ("Checkpoint," "Halloween"). Walking late at night through public space can bring on a mauling from a werewolf or exsanguination from a vampire ("Phases," "Wild at Heart"). Strange entities such as giant snakes or skeletal demons lurk on Main Street ("Shadow," "Hush"). Homicide is a common extracurricular activity at Sunnydale High School ("Prophecy Girl," "Becoming, Part 1," 'Passion"). To complement the image of public space as threatening, when one is inside the home one is protected from the threat of vampires ("Passion," "Crush"). The reinforcement of the street as a place to be feared and the home as one of sanctuary is a discourse that reinforces patriarchal notions of where women should and should not be.

Although it often portrays a division between public and privates space,

Buffy the Vampire Slayer provides an important tool in combating that hegemony. Buffy is active in appropriating public space. The fear she experiences on a nightly basis does not limit her movement in public places. The dissolution of patriarchal constructions of public and private spaces serves as a televisual example of "public privates." This is evidenced by the complex and paradoxical geographies portrayed on *Buffy the Vampire Slayer.*

The power behind television programs like *Buffy the Vampire Slayer* is in its emancipatory possibilities. It actively seeks to disrupt gendered behavioral stereotypes. For Douglas Kellner, "Emancipatory popular culture subverts ideological codes and stereotypes, and shows the inadequacy of rigid conceptions that prevent insight into the complexities and changes of social life."[40] During its seven seasons, *Buffy the Vampire Slayer* helped to challenge those ideological codes and stereotypes. Not only did Buffy have a romantic cross-species relationship with Angel and Spike (both vampires), so did her best friends Willow (with a werewolf) and Xander (with a former revenge demon). When Willow's relationship with her werewolf boyfriend Oz ended, she began a long-term lesbian relationship.

Although "no one television show or series can radically change consciousness or alter behavior, television can cause an individual to question previous beliefs, values, and actions. Such a process contains the potential for more significant subsequent changes."[41] Television doesn't have to show the "same old, same old" of Betty baking a Bundt cake in her deluxe kitchen with Whirlpool appliances (see my discussion of classic television programs). Television shows Buffy walking through a graveyard at night looking for a vampire to stake. It shows women no longer content with following prescribed societal rules of where they should go and where they should be. It shows an example of a woman transgressing patriarchal boundaries and refusing to be excluded.

Although it can play a role in upholding patriarchal notions of gender relations, the real power of television is in its potential to subvert those notions. Television can have an emancipatory quality in which it destabilizes traditional gender roles or deconstructs hegemonic discourse. Television may not lead the revolution, but it most definitely can play a part.

John Fiske writes: "The arguments that television is always an agent of the status quo are convincing, but not totally so. Social change does occur, ideological values do shift, and television is part of this movement. It is wrong to see it as an originator of social change, or even to claim that it ought to be so, for social change must have its roots in material social existence; but television can be, must be, part of that change, and its effectivity will either hasten or delay it."[42]

It will never be determined which has the greater influence, television on society or society on television. But it must be acknowledged that television is a powerful cultural tool that affects our daily life, including our identities and our perceptions of space and place. For "television is the *one* factor that practically all of the individuals in this society have in common. It is the unifying substratum of experience."[43]

Although it can be said that the claims for television's emancipatory power within this chapter is idealistic, I conclude by recounting an anecdote of one instance in which *Buffy the Vampire Slayer* provided a liberatory moment. On one of the Listservs to which I subscribed in doing research for this chapter, a story was posted from a British paper in which a young British teenager was confronted by a group of similarly aged young men in a parking garage of a shopping establishment. These men attempted to assault her, but their efforts were thwarted for she was able to defend herself. She had enrolled in self-defense courses after watching episodes of *Buffy the Vampire Slayer*. This young woman used television to provide her own emancipatory moment.

2

Home Is Where the Heart Is

Fast and Furious Geographies

Fast girls, faster cars. Perhaps that's what comes to mind when you read the words "the Fast and the Furious." Hot rods and hot bods are the backbone of the franchise. Feminists and action film lovers often find themselves in an ambiguous position. The relationship between feminism and action films is often a complicated one that is embroiled in paradox. Action movies have long been criticized for their objectification of women and their misogynistic tones. They often glorify masculinist attitudes toward women, but the patriarchal stance does not stop there. Many times, there is a hypermasculinization of men as well. Using examples from five of seven *Fast and Furious* films, this chapter discusses the franchise by showing how the series portrays gendered and cultural geographies.

Feminist analysis of media adds much to critical conversations on popular culture. Not only is the depiction of hegemonic stereotypes of femininity important to analyze, but dominant portrayals of masculinity should be examined as well. Geographers such as Peter Jackson, Lawrence Berg, and

Robyn Longhurst, along with other gender scholars, have discussed depictions of masculinity in media, but more research should be conducted.[1] Media "carries and exploits discourses of gender and gender inequalities in ways which frequently replicate uncritically the gendered values in the wider society and culture."[2]

As we have seen with *Buffy the Vampire Slayer*, popular culture has great potential to destabilize patriarchy, and yet mainstream media often reinforce patriarchal structures despite the occasional subversive attempt. Mass media fortify the framework that there are gender roles for the sexes to follow through the portrayal of characters, their interaction with others, and the activities they perform in the spaces they occupy.

We will look at five of the seven films in the *Fast and Furious* franchise (the seven comprise Universal Studio's largest franchise in terms of box office gross), omitting *2 Fast 2 Furious* (2003) and *The Fast and the Furious: Tokyo Drift* (2006). Those selected for analysis are *The Fast and the Furious* (2001), *Fast & Furious* (2009), *Fast Five* (2011), *Fast & Furious 6* (2013), and *Furious 7* (2015).[3] My methodological approach to these films is to discuss them as a film franchise rather than as separate and discrete works.

Reel/Real Worlds

Film is a popular and powerful medium that reaches billions of people each year. Whether the movie is watched in a theater, at home, or on a mobile device, there is an interaction between the medium and the audience. A dialectical relationship exists between the viewer and the film—one's identity informs how a message is interpreted and the message influences one's identity.

While the *Fast and Furious* films cannot be viewed as a substitute for the real world due to their fantastic nature, I take them as empirical examples of social constructions. They are not supposed to mirror real life. The *Fast and Furious* franchise is based on over-the-top action movies, but gender representations in these types of movies can still resonate with audiences.

The franchise, while by no means cinematic masterpieces, can show that blockbuster films do not have to be "deep" to bring out social change. Media representations have very real effects on real life. Even if a film is supposed to be an exaggerated spectacle, such as with these films, they can reject stereotypes and take on the difficult work of creating something that actually challenges what we think we know about people based on race, class, and gender.

Media shape not only our perceptions of reality, but also our relations with one another. They provide templates on how to act according to one's role and setting.[4] Media stories provide the symbols, myths, and resources through which we constitute a common culture and through the appropriation of which we insert ourselves into this culture. Media are "an integral part of popular culture and, as such, an essential element in molding individual and social experiences of the world and in shaping the relationship between people and place."[5] Film plays a large role in how we understand the world around us, whether it be immediate surroundings and situations or those more distant.

Movies, as representations of space, need to be studied more by geographers. Here I am not using Henri Lefebvre's notion of "representations of space," which are abstract, conceptualized spaces that make up planes of conception, but rather arguing that film is a unique opportunity to explore the socio-spatial dialectic by examining the space within the filmic text and the behaviors of the actors within that space.[6] Represented space has, of course, formal properties of physical space, and its relations to the world of represented events is the same as that of physical space to the world of physical events.[7] Film, as used in media geographies, "allows investigation of the production of dominant ideologies; and a site of resistance, in which the stability of any meaning is open to critical scrutiny".[8] There is room in media to both concretize and destabilize patriarchal ideologies and socio-spatialities.

The Fast and the Furious

Because the events of one film bleed into the next, I will discuss the *Fast and Furious* as a collection of stories instead of analyzing them film by film. Most of the events of *2 Fast 2 Furious* and *Tokyo Drift* are omitted because they deviate from the main story arc.

The series begins with undercover Los Angeles police officer Brian

O'Conner as he investigates ex-convict Dominic "Dom" Toretto and his crew because of their suspected involvement in the thefts of tractor-trailers carrying electronic equipment. We are introduced to Dom and his team at the Toretto garage/restaurant. Brian gains access to the team by ingratiating himself to Dom by saving him from arrest after an illegal street race. Owing Toretto a "ten-second car" because he destroyed the one promised after losing the street race, Brian and the rest work together to restore a Toyota Supra. Throughout the first film, Brian dates and then falls in love with Dom's sister, Mia. He eventually confesses his undercover status to her in order to save Dom and his band from the newly armed truck drivers. After an encounter with a shot-gunned driver, Brian discloses that he is an undercover cop to the crew. While Brian is attending to a wounded member of the team by calling for a medevac, Dom and the rest flee the scene. As Brian chases Dom through the streets of Los Angeles, Dom ends up colliding with a semi-truck, hurting himself and totaling his classic Dodge Charger in the process. Brian decides to let him go and hands Dom the keys to the Supra, stating, "I owe you a ten-second car."

While *2 Fast 2 Furious* is not analyzed here, an important plot point occurs in that film. U.S. Federal Bureau of Investigation (FBI) agents arrest Brian because he let Toretto flee. He is offered a deal to avoid a criminal record. Brian accepts the offer to go undercover again to capture a drug lord. He is successful in his pursuit and his record is expunged.

Meanwhile in the Dominican Republic, Dom and his new gang (including longtime girlfriend, Letty, from the original *The Fast and the Furious*) have abandoned electronics for hijacking fuel tankers. Feeling pressure from law enforcement and that the lifestyle was too dangerous, Dom leaves Letty in the Dominican Republic and heads to Panama. Dom soon receives the news that Letty has been murdered following a car accident running drugs for a dealer named Braga. Letty was actually working undercover in Braga's cartel in exchange for Dom's freedom. Dom and Brian soon reunite (albeit initially in a hostile manner) to infiltrate Braga's operation and get revenge for Letty's murder. After Braga is apprehended, Brian encourages Dom to run to escape prison, but Dom refuses. He is sentenced to twenty-five years to life for his crimes.

Brian, now reunited with Mia, frees Dom from the bus transporting him to prison. After the rescue, the three end up in Rio de Janeiro, Brazil. Mia reveals she is pregnant with Brian's child. In Brazil, they become involved with an operation to steal cars from a train. Realizing the cars are property of the U.S. Drug Enforcement Agency (DEA), Dom, Brian, and Mia abort the hijacking, but not before three DEA agents are killed by other members of the operation. Mia flees the scene in a Ford GT40 and crime boss Reyes captures Brian and Dom. Dom, Brian, and Mia are wrongly blamed for the murder of the DEA agents. A team of U.S. Diplomatic Security Service (DSS) agents led by Luke Hobbs is employed to bring them to back to the U.S. In the Ford GT40 Mia drove off of the train, Dom, Brian, and Mia find a chip detailing Reyes's criminal empire. This sparks a plan to steal one hundred million dollars of Reyes's money in order to start a new life in a country without extradition to the United States. In order to pull off the heist, they assemble a team consisting of characters from the original movie, *2 Fast 2 Furious*, *Tokyo Drift*, and *Fast & Furious*: Vince, Roman, Tej, Han, Leo, Santos, and Gisele. Hobbs eventually arrests Dom, Brian, and Vince in the favelas of Rio de Janeiro. Reyes's men, who are seeking revenge for the stolen chip, attack the DSS convoy. Members of Hobbs's team are killed in the battle in the streets as is Dom's childhood friend, Vince. To avenge his team's deaths, Hobbs and his Brazilian police partner, Elena, agree to assist Dom's crew in wiping out Reyes's fortune. Dom and his gang—with the help of Hobbs and Elena—pull off the heist by stealing Reyes's vault from the police station where it was kept. The team proceeds to drag the vault through the streets of Rio de Janeiro, cutting a wide path of destruction. Reyes follows in hot pursuit, but is eventually shot dead by Hobbs. Hobbs then offers Dom's team a twenty-four-hour head start before he pursues to arrest them in order to complete his assignment.

After they leave Rio de Janeiro, Dom and the rest of the crew go their separate ways. Settled in the Canary Islands, Mia and Brian now have a son named Jack, and Dom is involved with Elena, the Brazilian cop who pursued him in *Fast Five*. Hobbs—with his new partner Riley Hicks—asks Dom for his assistance on a case that needs Dom's (and his crew's) skill set. Dom agrees to help only after Hobbs reveals that Letty (who was supposedly murdered in *Fast & Furious*) is alive and working for the prime suspect, Owen Shaw. The gang (consisting of Brian, Han, Gisele, Tej, and Roman) reassembles in London. Mia stays in Spain to care for Jack. In return for their help, Hobbs guarantees full amnesty for their past crimes. After finding Shaw (and an amnesiac Letty), the gang works to stop him from building and selling a powerful weapon. Dom pursues Letty at every chance to try to save her from Shaw's grip and restore her memory. Eventually Shaw is captured, but released after he reveals he kidnapped Mia. Riley, Hobbs's partner, discloses she is working with Shaw and leaves with the villain. Letty decides to stay with Dom and his crew although her memories have not returned. In an epic showdown with Shaw, the gang tries to bring down his plane with their vehicles. Gisele dies in the attempt, saving romantic partner Han. Han and their friends are heartbroken. Letty kills Riley and Dom is able to secure the key component of Shaw's weapon after putting him in a coma and securing amnesty. Back in Los Angeles, Elena decides that Dom belongs with Letty and returns to Brazil to resume working on the police force.

Setting up the events of *Tokyo Drift* (as *Tokyo Drift* supposedly takes place after the events of *Fast & Furious 6*), Owen Shaw's brother, Deckard, kills Han in Tokyo and warns Dom that he's next. Vowing revenge for his brother, Deckard Shaw sets off to destroy Dom and Hobbs.

Dom and Letty work on trying to recover her memory and go to Race Wars in the desert to see if it will spark any memories. She races, but then drives away. Dom finds her and she bids him good-bye stating that she is no longer the Letty he knew. Letty stops him because she thinks the person she used to be is no longer who she is to Dom, and she doesn't want to hurt him anymore.

Meanwhile, Deckard Shaw breaks into Hobbs's office to gather information on Dom's crew. Shaw and Hobbs battle for a while and when it seems like Hobbs has the upper hand, Shaw throws a grenade and seriously harms Hobbs. Elena, who has been working with Hobbs and was also in the office at the time of Shaw's attack, is unscathed.

Dom arrives at the old Toretto home as Brian and again pregnant Mia are getting their son ready for school. Outside the home is a large package addressed to Dom. While the siblings are talking, Dom gets a call from Deckard Shaw. Realizing they are all in danger, Dom shields Mia as the package explodes and destroys the Toretto house. The explosion injures no one. Dom learns from Hobbs the identity of Deckard Shaw and about Shaw's training in which he was turned into a "human killing machine." Dom vows to Hobbs that he will deal with Deckard Shaw and protect his family. Brian, Tej, Roman, and Letty reunite to take down Deckard Shaw via a newly invented surveillance system. Back in Los Angeles after a bit of globetrotting, Dom finds Deckard Shaw and they battle in the streets. Hobbs—alerted to Dom's predicament—leaves his hospital bed to help. Dom and Hobbs defeat Shaw and he is incarcerated in a maximum-security "black site" facility. Letty recovers her memory and tells Dom that she remembers their marriage in the Dominican Republic before he left.

After the action ends, the "family" is together again. Dom, Letty, Tej, and Roman watch Brian, a pregnant Mia, and son, Jack, play in the sand. While Brian does not state he's retiring, it is inferred as we see the saddened team discussing how "things will be different" in the future. Dom eventually leaves without saying goodbye. As he drives away, Brian catches him and they begin to race as they do. Dom and Brian race until at a fork in the road. Dom drives one way while Brian drives another.

In a touching tribute to the late actor Paul Walker (Brian) who died in November 2013, Dom remembers his adventures with Brian as their last film together concludes.

> DOM: I used to say I live my life a quarter mile at a time and I think that's why we were brothers—because you did too. No matter where you are, whether it's a quarter mile away or halfway across the world. You'll always be with me. And you'll always be my brother.

Fast and Furious Feminism

Media scholars have praised the franchise for its racial and ethnic diversity. While the praise is not universal (see critical analysis of skin tone in *Fast Five* below), the majority of what is written about the *Fast and Furious* films discusses their "racelessness" as many cast members are nonwhite/multiracial.[9]

Very little has been written about gender and the *Fast and Furious* franchise. Most of the analysis found in research was in the form of blog and newspaper reviews. Although critics of *Fast Five* responded mostly in a positive manner, some criticized the treatment of women: "[Females] cameo strikingly in buttock form. Others actually have first names."[10] *Variety* focused on the characters of Dom and Hobbs, who harken back to the "brawny" leading men of the 1980s (like Schwarzenegger and Stallone) and of the "manly men" typical of the 1950s and 1960s, calling their presence in *Fast Five* "a welcome injection of tough-guy vigor."[11] Another blogger describes the franchise thusly: "I was consumed by issues of race in F & F, until a friend mentioned 'I liked that the women could drive.' It was a delightful observation about the counter-stereotypical presentation of gender in the film. Throughout the franchise, women have always had very impressive road skills. There is no 'damsel in distress,' a helpless female character who cannot drive. Driving is the great equalizer in F & F, and although women are still contextualized as love interests, they are considered to be indispensable members of the team."[12]

Women in the *Fast and Furious* films are part of the crew. They are not seen as different because they are women. Mia and Letty are integral to the action of the films, while Gisele plays important roles in the series as well. Not because they need to be rescued (with one exception in *Furious 7*), but because they are part of the group. Elena is portrayed as a proficient police officer and Riley is a force of impressive fighting ability with whom to be reckoned in her role as a double agent (eventually becoming a villain) during *Fast & Furious 6*. These fast and furious women can, and will, contribute their skill set to whatever job needs to be done.

However, there is a paradoxical portrayal of women in the films. For instance, in an early scene in *The Fast and the Furious*, a racer is offered an additional "trophy" if he wins:

[Monica runs Edwin's hand over her breast before the race]
MONICA: Feel that? This is yours, even if you lose. But if you win, you get her too.
[Edwin races and loses]

EDWIN: Hey, hey, Monica!
MONICA: What's your problem, nigga? You didn't win!
[Crowd mocks Edwin]

In another scene a woman is compared to a car. Dom says to team member Jesse: "Take it upstairs, Einstein! You can't detail a car with the cover on." Furthermore, when Letty approaches Elena at the end of *Fast & Furious 6*, Tej and Roman run a sexist commentary:

TEJ: This is gonna be awkward . . .
TEJ/ROMAN: . . . but sexy as hell!

As these scenes exhibit, there are a number of contradictions in the portrayal of women within the films.

While I argue that the franchise is feminist in some aspects, the series does not pass one key cultural test: the Bechdel-Wallace Test. In order for a film to pass the Bechdel-Wallace Test (a test created by Alison Bechdel and Liz Wallace), it has to have the following components:

1. It has to have at least two named women in it,
2. who talk to each other,
3. about something besides a man.

The test first appeared in Bechdel's comic strip in 1985 and is inspired by Wallace's reading of the following Virginia Woolf passage from chapter five of *A Room of One's Own*:

But how interesting it would have been if the relationship between the two women had been more complicated. All these relationships between women, I thought, rapidly recalling the splendid gallery of fictitious women, are too simple. So much has been left out, unattempted. And I tried to remember any case in the course of my reading where two women are represented as friends. . . . They are now and then mothers and daughters. But almost without exception they are shown in their relation to men. It was strange to think that all the great women of fiction were, until Jane Austen's day, not only seen by the other sex, but seen only in relation to the other sex. And how small a part of a woman's life is that. . . . Suppose, for instance, that men were only represented in literature as the lovers of women, and were never the friends of men, soldiers, thinkers, dreamers; how few parts in the plays of Shakespeare could be allotted to them; how literature would suffer![13]

The test has been described as "the standard by which feminist critics judge television, movies, books, and other media."[14] Yet a movie can easily pass the Bechdel-Wallace Test and still be incredibly misogynistic. According to Neda Ulaby of National Public Radio, the test rings true because "it articulates something often missing in popular culture: not the number of women we see on screen, but the depth of their stories, and the range of their concerns."[15] The *Fast and Furious* franchise does not always pass the Bechdel-Wallace Test, yet the films have feminist elements and treat male and female characters equitably.

Think for a moment about the words "fast" and "furious." They evoke images of action, of aggression. Aggression has been traditionally viewed as a masculine characteristic, yet the women in these films are fast and furious. This ideology that is built into the heart of the franchise begins to undermine conventional notions of gendered behavior. Examples of both the reification and destabilization of gender norms within the films start with the character of Letty.

Depictions of Femininity

Letty Ortiz is a strong female character, both physically and mentally. Letty is Dom's longtime girlfriend, but she is not solely defined by that role (although that is her introduction).

> MIA: Letty lived just down the street. Always into cars though. Ever since she was like ten years old. So naturally, Dom always had her attention. Then she turned sixteen . . .
> BRIAN: . . . and she had Dom's.

She is a key member of the crew; Letty is critical to the heists in *The Fast and the Furious* and *Fast & Furious*. She is also one of the main storylines of *Fast & Furious 6*.

Letty is also portrayed as a woman that prominently displays and owns her sexuality, but the representation of her sexuality is not monolithic. To diffuse a tense situation at a house party, she tells Dom, "You look a bit tired . . . I think you should go upstairs and give me a massage," when he is angered by the actions of his friends. Letty has no problem "marking her territory" and establishing her strong presence. When surrounded by a group of scantily clad women waiting for a street race to start, she asserts her dominance with the following: "I smell [sniffs air] skanks. Why don't you girls just pack it up before I leave tread marks on your face?" Her treatment of other women, while not progressive by any means, shows a tough exterior needed by someone in her lifestyle. When hit on at a race, Letty replies, "You want a piece of ass, go to Hollywood Boulevard. You want an adrenaline rush that'll be two large." These quotes demonstrate how Letty is a complicated character. She often objectifies women competing for Dom's attention, but she is also confident in her relationship with him.

She is also assured in her abilities to race. In the following exchange with Dom during *Fast & Furious 6*, amnesiac Letty brags about her racing skills while Dom tries to trigger her memories of them together:

LETTY: You got some serious balls, man. [a microaggression][16]

DOM: I've been told.

LETTY: You know you're lucky I missed my shot. [Letty shot him in the shoulder in an earlier scene]

DOM: I think you hit your mark.

LETTY: Really . . . what is it with you? What, have you got a death wish or something?

DOM: If that's what it takes. I just wanna race.

LETTY: Might lose your car.

DOM: Let's do it.

LETTY: Your funeral.

DOM: Ride or die, remember?

As one might see from these exchanges, Letty is not a meek woman but instead quite brash. She holds her own when confronted. For example, during a conflict she taunts a villainous colleague with, "Klaus, aren't you Team Muscle? Don't make me go over there and make you Team Pussy." While this microaggression should not be ignored, it is further evidence of Letty's somewhat harsh personality. It's interesting that while she can be abrasive, she is only once referred to as a "bitch"—as "one tough bitch" by Owen Shaw. Her hard exterior is critiqued only in this one instance. This is unusual in film today—often strong female characters are denigrated for their nonconformance to stereotypical gender roles.

She is not necessarily a feminist figure because of these characteristics, but Letty does a lot to break down gendered stereotypes of action movies—she is not a damsel in distress, she is not simply the eye candy to satisfy a predominantly male audience. To counter that, some might argue that she is not a feminist figure because of her dominant physical presence and use of microaggression. She could be seen as, to use Yvonne Tasker's term, "musculinized."[17] But even that musculinization can destabilize gendered stereotypes by "restaging the relationship between women and violence as not only one of danger in which women are objects of violence but also a pleasurable one in which women retaliate to become the agents of violence and turn the table on their aggressors."[18]

Further musculinization occurs with the addition of Riley Hicks (portrayed by mixed martial arts [MMA] fighter Gina Carano) in *Fast & Furious 6* and *Furious 7* with a cameo role by MMA fighter Ronda Rousey. The characters of Mia and Gisele balance this musculinization. While not as physically imposing as Letty or Riley, they are still experienced and essential members of the team.

Mia is initially set up as the "desirable" sister of Dom who works at the family business and not much more. She quickly becomes part of a love triangle between Brian and Dom's friend, Vince. She only has feelings for Brian despite Vince's attraction to her. In the following exchange, Brian is questioned by his fellow police officers about his growing attraction for her in *The Fast and the Furious*:

TANNER: Are you going native on me, Brian?

MUSE: I think the sister's clouding his judgment.

BRIAN: What was that?

MUSE: Hey, I don't blame you. I get off on her surveillance photos too.

Her role as object (and I use that word deliberately) of affection soon shifts as the film series progresses. I use "object" because she is not a well-rounded or developed character until later in the franchise.

Although Mia is a skilled racing driver (her father was a race car driver), she avoids entanglement in Dom's illegal schemes until he is sent to prison. Both Brian and Mia break him out of the prison bus in *Fast Five* and she begins her life on the lam as a criminal fugitive. Mia later establishes herself as a surveillance and intelligence expert. While not as physical a presence as Letty, she proves herself a vital member of the team through both her driving abilities and computer skills.

When Mia announces her pregnancy in *Fast Five*, she doesn't slow down. Her pregnancies (and her eventual child, Jack) become a plot point in *Fast & Furious 6* and *Furious 7*, but she still actively participates. She is not defined by her role as mother, but it does influence some decisions that she and Brian (as well as Dom) make throughout the film. For one, in *Fast Five*, they decide that the "job" they pull off in Rio de Janeiro (robbing a notorious crime boss) will be their last. As Mia goes into labor, Dom and Brian discuss the future:

NUN: Señor O'Conner, Señor O'Conner, hurry, come! Come! This way! This way!

ELENA: [to nun] It's all right, I've got it. [to Brian] It's okay, you're just in time.

DOM: You're gonna be a great father, Brian.

BRIAN: What makes you so sure?

DOM: Because I'll be there to kick your ass if you ain't. Get in there.

ELENA: Go.

DOM: Brian. Remember, the second you go through those doors, everything changes. Our old life is done.

One character, that of Gisele (played by Gal Gadot—the Wonder Woman of Patty Jenkins's 2017 film), is especially a paradox. In *Fast & Furious*, viewers are introduced to Gisele. She coordinates Braga's runners and designs their routes. She is the point person for Braga's racers. This demonstrates her skill in driving and her intelligence. Gisele is strong and accomplished, but sexualized. She is often objectified for her looks and body, yet she is an expert in driving and weapons. Roman ogles her in one of her first scenes in *Fast Five*:

ROMAN: Sexy legs, baby girl. What time do they open?
GISELE: [pulls her gun on Roman] They open at the same time I pull this trigger. Want me to open them?

In one scene she states, "You don't need to send a man to do a woman's job," as she uses her bikini-clad body to capture the handprint of Reyes (he places his hand on her bum and her bikini registers the print).

She becomes involved with Han Seoul-O in *Fast Five*. After watching Gisele drive, Han moons: "I think I'm in love." While Roman often chides Han for their relationship, he refrains from teasing Gisele. This demonstrates how men are seen as weak for being romantic and women are not. Scenes that depict Han as weak for caring promote a certain type of masculinity, which can be detrimental to viewers' identity formation and encourage harmful cultural norms.

ROMAN: [speaking to Han] I don't know, man. That was disrespectful. And I don't like the way she said it, like, [imitates Gisele] "He's a man." "He's a man"? So, what are we?
HAN: C'mon, she's just doing her job.
ROMAN: "Doing her job." I see what's going on.
HAN: See what?
ROMAN: You got the little stardust in your eyes, eh? Little birds floating around a bit. You don't want to lease this model. You want to buy.[19]
HAN: Can you please stop talking?
ROMAN: No, no, you're in love! Look at you! [laughs]
HAN: Just stop.

Portrayals of Masculine Ideals

The character of Roman is—by far—the most sexualized and sexist character developed in the franchise. Originator of the term "hoasis" in the films, he states his motivation for assisting in the Rio heist in *Fast Five*: "Eleven million? Sounds like a whole lot of vaginal activity to me." Roman incessantly makes comments about women's bodies as well as asserting a masculinity that denigrates other men for having romantic feelings about women. Roman objectifies women and sees them as commodities to be purchased with the money he gets from the heists.

Roman's masculinity is based on his sexuality. But his is not the only type of masculinity shown throughout the film. Han and Brian are more thoughtful men, while Dom and Hobbs seem to establish their masculinity through muscle mass. Dom is sensitive when it comes to family; beneath the brawny exterior a softer side exists. Dom and Hobbs are hypermasculine figures in the films.

Ben-Zeev et al. argue in their discussion of the psychology of communication in film: "Perhaps the most poignant prototype of masculinity as a negation of femininity is the *hypermasculine* man, depicted in a plethora of popular culture media. The hypermasculine male is characterized by the idealization of stereotypically masculine traits, such as virility and physicality, while concurrently rejecting traits seen as feminine and thus perceived as antithetical and even inferior to machismo, such as compassion or emotional expression."[20] This type of hypermasculinity occurs regularly in the *Fast and Furious* films, but is counterbalanced by other characters' actions and dialogue. For instance, Han (after seeing the other guys fighting with each other) stays out of the fray and quips: "I thought cockfights were illegal in Rio." As mentioned earlier, the characters of Hobbs and Dom (and obviously the actors who play them) are massive entities of muscle and brawn. Less physical and more sensitive characters such as Han balance them.

In demonstrations of their lack of physical skills, female characters are shown as more proficient and powerful than Han and Roman. This can aid in both the destabilization and concretization of gendered norms. For example, Letty and Riley battle in *Fast & Furious 6* on a number of occasions. In one scene they fight publicly in the London subway. This physical fight, in which each of the women are more than capable at hand-to-hand combat, is juxtaposed with Han and Roman fighting with one of Shaw's men. Even though it is a two-on-one fight, they are portrayed as inept at fighting and the scenes are spliced together to demonstrate just how powerful Letty and Riley are. After Riley handcuffs one of Letty's wrists, Letty uses the cuffs as makeshift brass knuckles, while Han and Roman stumble and bumble through their fight and are visibly hurt in the aftermath.

Sexuality

Key couples to the franchise are Mia and Brian (*The Fast and the Furious, Fast & Furious, Fast Five, Fast & Furious 6, Furious 7*), Dom and Letty (*The Fast and the Furious, Fast & Furious 6, Furious 7*), Han and Gisele (*Fast Five* and *Fast & Furious 6*), and—one might argue—the friendship of Brian and Dom (*The Fast and the Furious, Fast & Furious, Fast Five, Fast & Furious 6, Furious 7*). Mia and Brian become a couple in the original film, break up when Mia finds out that Brian is an undercover police officer, then get back together in *Fast & Furious*. Dom and Letty have been a couple since she was sixteen. After Letty "dies" in *Fast & Furious*, Dom becomes involved with Elena, despite Elena initially hunting Dom with Hobbs in *Fast Five*. While heterosexuality is the norm in these films, *Fast Five* also features Leo and Santos, a homosexual couple. For the most part, the displays of male and female bodies interacting reinforce heteronormativity.

Bloggers online have debated the intersection of race and sexuality in the films, especially in the later installments (*Fast Five, Fast & Furious 6, Furious 7*). *Fast Five* is the first movie in the franchise in which characters from all of the preceding films interact. Roman (the character with the darkest skin color) is often portrayed as a selfish man who is only into money and the women that money can attract. He is often making comments that highlight a "player" attitude and a hypersexual mentality. In *2 Fast 2 Furious*, in which Roman is introduced, he says, "Man, it's a hoasis in here," to describe the women at a club. This is a problematic way to frame a character as it conveys negative cultural and racial stereotypes.

On the blog "Gradient Lair," the original poster describes an interaction between Roman and Han, who is Korean: "There is a very uncomfortable scene [in which] 'Roman' talks to 'Han' [and alludes] to penis size and sexual satisfaction and mocks 'Han' for loving 'Giselle' [*sic*] . . . [The] large penis and too immature for love stereotype [is associated] with the darkest Black male character 'Roman,' and is a common stereotype of Black men."[21] For example:

> ROMAN: You got special plans? Big day? You're going to invite us all out? Better make sure you get her a big rock, man, 'cause she doesn't look like she'll be that easily impressed. And if it's not a big rock, you better be big somewhere else. You know what I'm talking about? [laughs, then nudges Han]
>
> HAN: That's why all your girlfriends wear so much bling, huh?

The blog continues with: "Media is not arbitrary, random, neutral or apolitical. The characters could have been presented . . . without resorting to old stereotypes and racial hierarchies. It doesn't matter if the film was not meant to be 'deep.' Human lives are. Media characterizations have very real repercussions for real life. Even a film meant to be 'just fun' can reject stereotypes and take on the difficult work of creating something that actually challenges what we think we know about people based on race."[22] The same is true for gender stereotypes, whether it be the damsel in distress or the hypermasculine action hero archetype. Gradient Lair's take on race is important to note as is the intersection of race and sexuality. Portrayals of sexuality in the franchise often reinforce dominant and problematic norms regarding constructions of masculinity, femininity, heteronormativity, and race.

Place plays an important role in the representations of both femininity and masculinity as well as of sexuality. The places shown in the *Fast and Furious* franchise are a mixture of public and private spaces. Private spaces include homes, garages, and hideouts, while the public places are typically the streets with the exception of the Toretto business.

Within the home, some stereotypical gender norming happens. For instance, in *The Fast and the Furious*, Mia is washing dishes in the kitchen while her brother and her friends watch movies. But there is a bit of disruption to the norm when Brian comes in and offers to help her, stating, "Where I come from, the cook doesn't do the dishes." Mia also serves food in the restaurant portion of the Toretto garage. Her domestic duties fall by the wayside in later films as she becomes a fugitive and her character develops into a proficient intelligence and logistics analyst.

The home can also be interpreted as a male refuge (similar to the notion discussed in "Visions of Gender"). The members of the team—including Letty who is often masculinized within the series—relax and party in the Toretto home. They have little to no domestic duties. The space of the home loses significance as the franchise progresses, but the importance of the idea of home increases.

The Toretto garage (featured heavily in the first film) is a masculinized place. The only female member ever seen within that space is Letty. But as mentioned above, she does not fit stereotypical gendering. Her presence in the garage and her proficiency with mechanical work can help to destabilize patriarchal gender norms.

The hideouts/hangouts are more neutrally gendered. Both men and women are seen as comfortable in the space and as equally belonging. The equalizer seems to be their talent and skills as members of the team. For example, the women are all accomplished. Letty is an excellent driver and fighter; Gisele is an expert with weapons as well as in driving; and Mia is the logistical coordinator for the team and an adept driver. In addition to driving, the men also have different skill sets (e.g., Tej is most intelligent; Roman is a smooth talker; and Dom provides the brawn). These places are collaborative, and within them, the team works together to problem solve the situation at hand.

The streets of *Fast and Furious* are complexly constructed in regard to patriarchal feminine norms. Women are trophies and sexualized, nameless bodies in some scenes, but they are also seen as proficient drivers. In all of the films, women are racers or drivers in the operations the team undertakes. The streets as a space of gender neutrality are explored further in the next section.

Fast and Furious Geographies

The multiple spatialities present in the franchise portray diverse geographies. The urban backdrops of the films highlight urban and cultural geographies and, at times, socioeconomic geographies. Films that focus on inner cities have been around since the 1920s.[23] Mary Beltrán argues: "These movies established an iconography of urban environments and narrative expectations that both reflected and reinforced hegemonic notions of race, ethnicity, and class tied to housing and perceived safety in the United States. For instance, nonwhite city dwellers in urban genre films of the 1960s are often presented as problem people engaged in criminal or violent activity or effectively powerless and victimized in the face of insurmountable social problems."[24]

In the 1970s, this shifted with the rise of martial arts films and blaxploitation movies that hoped to bring moviegoers (especially urban patrons) back to downtown theaters.[25] The *Fast and Furious* series is a descendent of this legacy, hybridizing genres and creating an "exploitation-style race car film, low-rider teen culture [film], the urban gang movie and the cop film."[26]

Contemporary films now reflect the changing racial and ethnic composition of the United States. Heroes are no longer solely white males, but diverse in socioeconomic identities. This subverts traditional stereotypes of gender, race, and class in the action genre. The multiracial Dom and the white Brian both reinforce and problematize the stereotype of the leading man. Both of the men are foci in the series and their relationship, although somewhat tense at times, is quintessentially a "bromance." They compete with one another (often in a friendly manner) throughout the franchise.

The cultural geographies present in the series focus on gender, sexuality, and race/ethnicity. These are important cultural and social components to understanding in an increasingly diverse world both in real and reel life. The most recurring geographic tropes within the films are based on territory/turf wars, equality in the streets, and "home is where the heart is."

Territory and Turf Wars

The setting in Los Angeles says much about the original film. Known for racial and ethnic diversity, urban scholars often tout Los Angeles as the site for both the American dream and urban nightmares.[27] Beltrán argues that *The Fast and the Furious* depicts Los Angeles as racially harmonious.[28] To some extent, this is true; but the movie also depicts a violent turf war between street racing gangs

In the first film, each gang protects their turf within the city and defends it from rival intrusion. This is seen repeatedly in scenes that show how territory is marked and how those who infringe are subject to violence. While Beltrán contends the competition is amicable between the gangs, calling it a "utopic subculture," there is bad blood between the Vietnamese racing gang and Dom's.[29] After multiple run-ins throughout the first film, Johnny Tran, leader of the Vietnamese racing gang, eventually kills a member of Dom's gang. After Johnny kills Jesse and shoots further at Dom and Brian, the duo chases Lance (Johnny's right-hand man) and Johnny through the streets of Los Angeles. Johnny is eventually killed when his motorcycle crashes.

Early in the film, Johnny Tran holds Dom and Brian at gunpoint:

JOHNNY: I thought we had an agreement. You stay away. I stay away. Everybody stays happy.
DOM: We got lost. What do you want me to tell you?

Johnny and his band then shoot up Brian's car and force Dom and Brian to walk back to Dom's house. The destroyed car is punishment for infringing on their turf.

The tension mounts between the rivals as Race Wars, an event held in the California desert in which drivers race each other for cash or pink slips, approaches:

JOHNNY: I'll see you in the desert next month. Be ready to have your ass handed to you.
DOM: You're gonna need more than that crotch rocket.
JOHNNY: I got something for you.

During Race Wars, Johnny Tran defeats Jesse, a member of Dom's team. Afterward, Johnny confronts Dom:

JOHNNY: [about Jesse who is driving away] Where's he going?

DOM: He went to the car wash.

JOHNNY: Whatever. Go fetch my car!

DOM: Go fetch your car? We're not on your block any more. You better watch who you talk to like that.

JOHNNY: [Dom walks away] TORETTO! TORETTO! SWAT came into my house, disrespected my whole family because somebody narc'd me out! And you know what? IT WAS YOU!

[Dom punches Tran and a brawl ensues]

DOM: I never narc'd on nobody! I never narc'd on nobody!

As Dom and Johnny brawl, Letty punches and knocks out Lance to prevent him from entering the fight. This scene is another example of turf wars and territoriality. In this scene—as opposed to the earlier confrontation on Johnny's block—Dom no longer has to defer to Johnny because they are not in Johnny's space as they were earlier in the film. Race Wars is a neutral space. It is neutral because it is a racing space. This neutrality and equality can be seen throughout the racing scenes of the movie.

In *The Fast and the Furious*, the streets are the racers' domain until police appear. At the first sound of sirens, racers scatter to the cars lining the streets. Police chase Dom through the streets until Brian picks him up and takes him back home to the "fort" where his crew is hanging out.

When Dom and Brian take the restored Toyota Supra out for a ride, they spy a Ferrari next to them. Brian compliments the car and asks about its price. When the driver responds that the cost is "more than you can afford," Dom says to Brian "Smoke him." The Supra and Ferrari race for a stretch and the Supra passes the more expensive sports car. The race is up the Pacific Coast Highway and they disregard traffic laws and endanger other drivers in their racing path.

In *Fast & Furious*, Brian plants methamphetamines on one of Braga's drivers in order to create an opening in the organization. Braga holds a race before deciding on his newest "runners." When one of the potential runners asks, "Who's closing the streets?," Campos [Braga] responds, "No one. That's the point." The racers go on to wreak havoc on the streets of Los Angeles. The streets are shown, once again, to be property of the racing subculture.

This coding of racing spaces carries over to *Fast Five* (set in Rio de Janeiro). Yet, in a sense, there is a power shift from the dominant authority of the DSS squad to the subculture of racing. As Hobbs tries to apprehend Dom and Brian in Brazil, he is met with resistance:

HOBBS: Hey Toretto, you're under arrest.

DOM: I don't feel like I'm under arrest. [to Brian] How about you, Brian?

BRIAN: No, not a bit. Not even a little bit.

HOBBS: Just give it a minute. It will sink in.

BRIAN: We didn't kill those feds. That was Reyes.

HOBBS: I don't give a shit. I'm just here to bring two assholes whose names hit my desk.

BRIAN: Yeah, that sounds like a real hero.

HOBBS: That's funny. From a guy who took the oath of a cop, then went against everything it stood for, for some wannabe tough guy prick who beat a man half to death with a socket wrench. Yeah, real tough. You turn around and put your hands behind your back.

DOM: I don't think so.

HOBBS: Your mistake is thinking you have a goddamn choice, boy!

DOM: And your mistake? Thinking you're in America. You're a long way from home. This is Brazil!

[Crowd pulls out guns and points them at DSS squad]

The racing subculture protects Dom and Brian. They have taken over the streets of Brazil and state authority is ineffectual. It is the racers' turf, not Hobbs's.

The cultural geographies resonate throughout the urban landscape of the films, whether Los Angeles, Rio de Janeiro, or London. Territory is significant to the racers and their teams and when that turf is transgressed, tension mounts, and violence breaks out. Transgressions of codes of conduct are not tolerated. There is an underlying set of norms for the subculture and that includes a sense of equality in the streets.

Equality in the Streets

Equality between racers is portrayed throughout the franchise despite the fact that they are racing against one another. Driving ability is key to earning respect. That respect garners status in the streets. While a hierarchy may exist, that hierarchy only discriminates based on racing ability. If one wins a race, that person is well-respected and regarded regardless of race, gender, or class as seen in the first organized racing scene of the franchise:

BRIAN: Hey, wait, hold up! I don't have any cash, but I do have the pink slip to my car.

JESSE: Wait, you just can't climb in the ring with Ali 'cause you think you can box!

BRIAN: [points to Vince with whom he had an earlier altercation] He *knows* I can box! So check it out, it's like this: If I lose, winner takes my car clean and clear. But if I win, I take the cash, *and* I take the respect!

DOM: [laughing] Respect?

BRIAN: To some people, that's more important.

Brian and Dom, along with two other racers, compete through the streets. Dom wins. When Brian brags that he "almost had Dom" after their first race, Dom laughs at his ignorance:

DOM: You almost had me? You never had me—you never had your car . . . Granny shiftin' not double clutchin' like you should. You're lucky that hundred shot of NOS didn't blow the welds on the intake! You almost had me?

EXTRA: You tell him Dom. Get out of here.

DOM: Now, me and the mad scientist got to rip apart the block . . . and replace the piston rings you fried.[closes hood of car] Ask any racer. Any real racer. It don't matter if you win by an inch or a mile. Winning's winning.

[Crowd cheers in agreement]

Dom Toretto, the protagonist of the *Fast and Furious* series, lives for racing:

DOM: I live my life a quarter mile at a time. Nothing else matters: not the mortgage, not the store, not my team and all their bullshit. For those ten seconds or less, I'm free.

For Dom, it is one's racing ability rather than one's socioeconomic status that matters. *The Fast and the Furious* echoes this as a representation of the racing subculture. In the first movie, the racers are diverse in race, class, and gender. Beltrán notes that "the extras in fact were actual street racers, and Asian Americans, Latinos, and African Americans far outnumber whites."[30]

Sexist tones do exist in many scenes, but others of empowerment counterbalance them. This is not to say that to be empowered women need to be able to drive fast cars, fight like a professional mixed martial artist, or have incredible aim with a weapon. But the *Fast and Furious* films do not treat women who can perform these acts as exceptions. I chose to investigate the *Fast and Furious* films for many reasons, but primarily because of their portrayals of women. When I first watched the movies, I was intrigued by characters that weren't singled out for being women, but instead were just part of the crew—admired not only for their looks but their abilities.

Stereotypes of femininity that the *Fast and Furious* women exhibit, and how that femininity plays into patriarchal standards of beauty, can be viewed in multiple ways. To some, those stereotypes can be viewed as contributing to conventional notions of femininity and beauty. They could be viewed as promoting idealized images of beauty that most women cannot attain.

The franchise portrays equality (regardless of one's race, class, or gender) as long as one is skilled. This can be a liberating way to approach gender in action films and get away from patriarchal and traditional norms in action films.

Home Is Where the Heart Is

The franchise continues to break conventional genre traits by focusing on the themes of family and home. The concept of family and place of home are important in the *Fast and Furious* world. The team gathers at the home for "family" dinners and other social events. Vince storms off after seeing Brian at the "family" barbeque. When he returns, they gather to say grace.

At the end of *Furious & Furious 6*, the family is assembled once again, recalling the original family dinner at the end of *The Fast and the Furious*. While the series is chided for being a bit sentimental and over the top with theme of family, it adds a much-needed element of emotion to the franchise.

When Dom suggests that the trio of Brian, Mia, and himself split up and go their separate ways in *Fast Five*, Mia tells the two men that she's pregnant. She goes onto to say, "I've already lost my family once. I'm not going through that again." As they celebrate the news, Dom states, "Our family just got bigger."

Also in *Fast Five*, Vince asks Dom if he can join the heist of $100 million from Reyes. Dom replies, "There's always room for family." As Vince is dying from wounds sustained from a shootout with Reyes's men in the favelas of Rio de Janeiro, he divulges that he named his son "Nico" after Dom(inic). After Vince dies, Dom mourns over his body: "You were always my brother." As the crew gathers together to pull off the vault heist, Dom toasts them with "Salud, mi familia." After the successful heist, he leaves Vince's share with Vince's wife and son.

In *Fast & Furious 6*, Hobbs tells Dom, "Make [your] family whole again," as he hands him a picture of Letty. Mia gives Brian and Dom her blessing to go after Letty.

MIA: We're family. We got a problem; we deal with it together . . . We're stronger together . . . Go get Letty, bring her home.

Brian and Dom discuss the Hobbs deal to go back to Los Angeles. Brian says, "It just doesn't feel like home" in the Canary Islands. They agree to assist Hobbs to get Letty back and to have the freedom to return to the United States.

In *Fast & Furious 6*, the theme of home occurs repeatedly. For instance, after the team hands over the Shaw's microchip/weapon, the following exchange transpires:

DOM: [Handing over the microchip to Hobbs] So this is worth billions.
HOBBS: Name your price, Dom.
DOM: 1327. [referring to the address of his home in LA]

Later in that film, Owen Shaw and Dom discuss how family is a weakness for Dom:

OWEN: A street kid, starts out stealing DVD players in East LA, ends up heisting $100 million in Rio.

DOM: Not bad, huh?

OWEN: It's a good story, isn't it? Almost inspiring. See, what I couldn't fathom is why he's not relaxing on a beach somewhere with that cute little Brazilian number. Instead, he's working with a two-bit government hack like Hobbs. And then I realized, he has a weak spot.

DOM: We all got a weak spot.

OWEN: You know, when I was young, my brother always used to say, "Every man has to have a code." Mine? Precision. A team is nothing but pieces you switch out until you get the job done. It's efficient. It works. But you? You're loyal to a fault. Your code is about family. And that's great in the holidays, but it makes you predictable. And in our line of work, predictable means vulnerable. And that means I can reach out and break you whenever I want.

DOM: At least when I go, I'll know what it's for.

OWEN: Well, at least you have a code. Most men don't. So, I'm going to give you a chance—take your crew and walk away. That's the only way you're going to keep your family safe.

DOM: Your brother never told you never to threaten a man's family? It's a pretty stupid thing to do. But I'll make it simple for you: I walk away when she [Letty] walks away.

Another example occurs when a still amnesiac Letty is brought back to the Toretto house. She is asked if anything seems familiar. She replies, "No, but it feels like home."

Furious 7 reinforces the concept of family. After the Toretto home is destroyed, the desire to protect his "family" motivates Dom to "one last ride." As Dom states early in the film, "I don't have friends. I got family." The main villain, Deckard Shaw, tells Dom:

DECKARD: You shouldn't have messed with my family.

[Toretto put his brother Owen Shaw in a coma in *Fast & Furious 6*]

DOM: I told your brother the same thing.

Furious 7 ends poignantly as the crew sees their last run with Brian. Because of Paul Walker's (the actor who portrays Brian) untimely death, Brian needed to retire although this is not explicitly spelled out. As the film ends, Dom and Brian take one last ride together. The film ends with the words "For Paul."

Family is the key theme of the *Fast and Furious* films. Home and family are subjects often featured in films, but not necessarily in the action genre due to patriarchal constructions of them as feminized spaces. In *Furious 6*, Mia stays home with her son, Jack, and Elena. This can be interpreted as another tie to the home for Mia. She is responsible for the home and childcare. This can reinforce the stereotype of the mother as the nurturer and "natural" caretaker for children, while the father leaves the home to "work."

While the home is sometimes portrayed as a burden for Mia and a refuge for Dom and his friends, all characters regardless of their gender share a sentimental attachment to the home. Geographies of home are prominent within the series and it lends a bit of heart to the films. Family is a motivating factor within the franchise. The home is an intimate space for family. The films, through their emphasis on home and family, undermine some of the masculinist tendencies of action films.

Geographies in Action

The *Fast and Furious* franchise is built on the draw of spectacle. The fantastic and unrealistic action scenes entertain the audiences and lead to box office billions. The films, however, can be seen as more than just stunts and dollars. There are feminist and cultural geographic elements to consider in the series.

The films, while they glorify stereotypes of femininity and masculinity in a patriarchal manner, also make some feminist arguments about equality and ability. Both male and female bodies glisten on screen, but the characters are more than just their corporeal frames. The female characters are developed to be more than objects; their abilities are highlighted repeatedly and are essential to the crew. Some male leads show sensitivity and emotion, which is not often portrayed in action films. The series repeatedly emphasizes the concept of family to humanize the characters. These two occurrences help to create a fast and furious feminism that can be seen as a thread throughout the franchise. The *Fast and Furious* films demonstrate that ability is more important than race, class, or gender.

Urban geographies can be seen in the territoriality of the gangs. When a rival turf is trespassed, negative repercussions ensue. This includes loss of property, but more importantly, loss of life. The gangs battle each other most explicitly in the first film—*The Fast and the Furious*—but elements can be seen throughout the franchise. In these films, the streets belong to the racers and they care nothing for the consequence of their actions on the roads. Mass destruction happens as the cars tear up cities that seem to get in the way of the drivers.

A less complicated argument regarding the films is the portrayal of cultural geographies. Depictions of race and ethnicity in the series both highlight racelessness and racial tensions. The franchise features a multiracial and diverse cast, but problematic elements can be shown in the portrayals of characters of color when it comes to sensitivity and sexuality.

The gendered and neutral depictions of public and private spaces within the series help to make the films a bit more complex in the messages transmitted to the viewing audience. The reel/real binary is still, of course, active in the films and in their eventual interpretations. The notion of public privates is important to bring into the analysis of the *Fast and Furious* films. It shows how spaces can both trouble and reinforce gendered constructions of filmic spatial representations.

3

Scared to Death

Spaces of J-Horror

Feminist Horror?

Horror films can be read in contradictory ways: they can uphold patriarchal dualisms and also depict the liberatory possibilities of subverting those binaries. Similar to action films, horror films are often criticized for their misogynistic messages.[1] Feminist media scholars object to the sexualized violence of many horror films (e.g., virginity is a life-saving characteristic whereas any form of sexual activity is a virtual death sentence). The almost "pornographic" feel of many horror texts is also criticized when sexual repression is acted out on women through bodily mutilation. While these arguments are merited, some feminist media scholars argue that horror films can help to destabilize patriarchal gender roles.[2] They argue that constrictive constructions of femininity are sometimes destabilized through the portrayal of a female protagonist or the "Final Girl." The Final Girl is proactive and defeats the killer/monster at the end, before the credits roll. She is the heroine of the film, not the victim. This is, however, not the case in every film, but as William Schoell states, "Scenes in which women whimper helplessly and do nothing to defend themselves are ridiculed by the audience, who find it hard to believe that anyone—male or female—would simply allow someone to kill them with nary a protest."[3] While the potential for subversion exists, it can be the case that the Final Girl upholds patriarchal dualisms to regain order at the conclusion of the Western horror film.

My aim is not to condemn horror films, but to investigate the sociospatial messages they convey. While the four films explored here can be read as potential destabilizations of patriarchal codings of space, they can also be read as ultimate reifications of those codings. Horror films transgress the boundaries of bodies and homes and violate the constructed division between interior/exterior, open/contained, and private/public.[4]

Feminist geographic investigation into horror films shows how portrayals of the body can influence understandings of abjection, often defined as a breakdown in the distinction of self and others or the disruption of corporeal reality, inciting feelings of disgust, unease, or horror. Investigations of the body lead to examinations of social norms as a whole. Increasingly, media texts are sites of exploration for geography, but interestingly, representations of horrific images on the screen have been largely left unstudied by geographers. Geographic inquiry into horror films is important not only because of the void in geographic knowledge, but also because understandings of space vary in horror texts. To this end, I will explore the difference between Western and Japanese horror themes.

J-Horror

New Asian Horror is a term that describes a specific type of Asian horror film originating with *Ringu* (1998). *Ringu* is a film widely considered to be the catalyst to the genre in the United States. More specifically, *Ringu* is the start of what is termed J-Horror, with the *J* standing for Japanese. New Asian Horror (which includes J-Horror as a subgenre) quite readily accepts monsters, supernatural powers, and the paranormal in general. This differs from traditional Western horror in which the "monsters" are often sociopaths or spaces of horror (e.g., in Western horror haunted houses or zombified bodies are often rejected as plausible entities).

Arguably, the most popular form of Western horror storytelling is based on the cautionary tale wherein characters are warned against doing something (yet they ignore said warning). They ultimately pay the highest cost for it—death. One of the larger issues with horror in the West is that it is usually bound to logic and morality. Concurrent with this is the necessity of establishing the monster/ghost/spirit's existence as something irrational that exists in a rational world. In short, the story must prove to the skeptic the existence of something fantastic.

In J-Horror, characters do not run from place to place, trying to escape a murderer. Instead, the audience follows the protagonist along a gradual, dread-filled path of mystery and self-discovery. The main character, usually a woman, often has a disturbing past that affects the present story. In J-Horror, many victims are quite literally "scared to death."

"J-Horror" is a cult-fan term that was meant as clarifying shorthand for previously hard to categorize films (in the West) like the *Ring* series, *Dark Water*, *Audition*, and *The Grudge*. Many J-Horror movies can trace their roots back to classical Japanese literature or performing arts. J-Horror is rooted in the two-thousand-year history of Japanese culture and traditions. For the most part, these films returned the horror genre back to the realm of the unseen terror and the psychological scare. J-Horror increasingly has impacted American horror movies, in part through remakes: *Ringu* was remade in America as *The Ring* (2002), *Ju-on* was remade as *The Grudge* (2004), and an American version of *Dark Water* was released in 2005. Another fan favorite, *Audition*, has yet to be reworked into a Western version.

So why did New Asian Horror, and especially J-Horror, take off? Some people argue that it's due to post–9/11 fear, but *The Grudge* star, William Mapother, discusses another stance:

> I don't know if it's because of changes in our culture or if some of the big studios are just now taking a chance on it and Americans would have been receptive to it a lot earlier. . . . Another possibility is that the

randomness of Japanese horror—in other words, there isn't a morality play as there is so often in American horror, characters punished for their sexuality or their greed. And I'm really going out on a limb here, but I wonder if because in Japanese horror, innocent people are victimized and a lot goes unexplained, if as a lot of cultural critics have pointed out, the last 15 years have produced as much fragmentation in our culture as they seem to have, then perhaps Americans are more accustomed and more open to things that aren't so easily explained or accounted for.[5]

Buddhism and Shinto adherents more easily accept the supernatural than do Judeo-Christian counterparts. Spirit coexistence with the living is not necessarily to be feared as the afterlife and the material worlds overlap. Shinto beliefs accept the supernatural or spirit world as part of the physical world. Many homes in Japan have a *butsudan*, an altar in which dead relatives are believed to "live." The supernatural simply is. The ghosts of these films are not defeated, they are not vanquished, but instead they continue on.

Hideo Nakata, a prominent J-Horror figure and director of *Ringu* and *Dark Water*, locates the difference between Japanese and Western horror films in religion and culture:

> The difference between Japanese horror and Western horror can be traced back to the difference in religious beliefs. When making horror films, the methods of describing the spiritual world and the expression of horror are totally different between Japan and the West. In a culture where the influence of monotheism such as Christianity is strong, the antinomy, or confrontation between the devil and God, becomes the fundamental conflict.[6]

In Japan, the spirits of those who die violently are typically believed to be unable to make their final passage to the world of the dead and reappear before the living until they fully avenge their deaths. In America and Europe, most horror movies tell the story of the extermination of evil spirits. Japanese horror movies end with a suggestion that the spirit still remains at large. The Japanese do not regard spirits only as enemies, but as beings that coexist with our world.

Many Hollywood studios chose to remake Japanese horror films about the avenging spirit or *obake*. Usually portrayed as a female entity, the spirit returns to the world of the living to exact vengeance upon those who harmed her. Films like *The Ring*, *The Grudge*, and *Dark Water* relate this tale of a wronged spirit. The look of the avenging spirit is much like it was in original Japanese horror films, dating back to the 1950s. It is usually a girl with long, black, unkempt hair, and typically a child that was brutally murdered. When she comes back, she wants her revenge on those who wronged her.[7]

These avenging-spirit stories may be what attract American viewers. Ghost stories can be scarier than serial killers, because ghosts are inescapable—and viewers notice the difference. For many fans of horror films, the difference is quite remarkable. Kristin Uyemura discusses how all J-Horror movies have to do with ghosts.[8] For the most part, Western horror is real people killing. It is more terrifying because if a spirit wants to kill you, nothing can be done. Nothing can fight off a ghost.

In the West, at least, horror stories were some of the earliest short films that were made. It was—quite simply—a way for filmmakers to get a response out of audiences in a short time. This ultimately translated into more money and that was much of the motivation that filmmakers needed. Even now, over one hundred years later, horror films perform better in a cost-benefit analysis than almost any other genre.

Japan, as it turns out, was not much different. What is different is how the audience viewed and continues to view horror. Japanese horror films are generally different from their U.S. counterparts in that they are primarily psychological in nature. A sense of trepidation, foreboding, and dread is created without resorting to the violent bloodletting and gore so common in American horror films. Roy Lee (producer of *The Ring* series, *The Grudge*, and *Dark Water*) analyzes the increasing popularity of Japanese horror films:

> Unlike American blood-and-gore horror movies, which are full of shocking images, J-horror films are characterized by stories that gradually raise the level of psychological fear as they unfold.... Some people say that the J-horror remake boom is the result of a shortage of effective ideas

in Hollywood, but I don't think so. The quality of Japanese movies has reached a level that is now competitive with the rest of the world. These and a number of other factors all came together at just the right time, and Hollywood, which is always looking for interesting films, opened its doors wide.[9]

Japanese fright flicks present their stories without making a clear delineation between good and evil, with the endings of such films sometimes being open-ended and inconclusive. As with real life, evil is not always vanquished.

Since ancient times, people in Japan have believed that ancestral spirits protect their descendants and daily life is carried out in the belief that spirits naturally dwell in close proximity. Many Japanese instinctively feel that there is an unseen world existing all around us. Japanese awareness of a spiritual world and their perceptions of horror are vastly different from those in Western cultures. In Japan, the burden of proof is not so high, and the average Japanese person is inclined to believe in ghosts because the culture is permeated with so many tales of them. Additionally, there is a belief that spirits inhabit almost everything from inanimate objects to living creatures, and if one is willing to believe in this, then one is willing to believe in the possibility of life after death. This blurring of lines between life and the afterlife can be the source of horror for many viewers. It creates unease and transgressions of spaces that unsettle one.

Abject Horror

Abjection is a useful theory with which to investigate horror films since the lack of structure or boundaries horrifies the viewer. Here I employ Julia Kristeva's mobilization of the term in which she defines abjection as a breakdown in the distinction between self and other and the horror one feels when corporeal reality is disturbed or transgressed.[10] Abject spaces are the spatial manifestation of the disruption of corporeal reality and considered dangerous and frightening because they are places of uncertainty. Boundaries dissolve in abject spaces, resulting in confusion of categories and apprehension as comfort levels are breached. Abjection encompasses the paradoxes of transgression, which is crucial to the critical examination of social relations and constructions.[11]

When limits are transgressed, when what is seen as normal suddenly becomes inverted, when bodies just will not die, when ghosts or monsters appear, when there is no safety, and everything is strange, abjection is felt. Elizabeth Grosz states that the abject is "what of the body falls away from it while remaining irreducible to the subject/object and inside/outside oppositions. The abject necessarily partakes of both polarized terms but cannot clearly be identified with either."[12] Abjection becomes a state more likely to occur when spatial boundaries are questioned.

As I have discussed in previous work, Barbara Creed, too, observes how horror texts can be used as an example of abjection.[13] Creed notes at least two ways. First, there are the images of abjection: putrefying flesh and bodily waste such as blood and vomit are ubiquitous in many horror films. The fear the films provoke can potentially violate bodily boundaries, as Creed points out when a viewer says that a film "scared the shit out of me."[14] Second, entities or people that cross boundaries or even threaten to cross them are seen as abject. These boundaries can be between bodily interior and exterior, public and private, living and dead, or good and evil.

Liminality is the state of being between—a threshold. Liminal spaces are those that exist in between binaries. The body can be a liminal space when it occupies both sides of binaries at the same time or is placed at the precipice of falling into one state or another. Liminality can easily lead to transgression.

The body in horror films is often depicted as a transgressive place. In J-Horror, as with other horror genres, the body is a liminal space that transgresses traditional boundaries between interior and exterior, public and private, and living and dead. In this chapter, I examine constructions of the body and home as liminal spaces in four J-Horror texts: *Ringu*, *Dark Water*, *Audition*, and *The Grudge*.

Understanding constructions of the body is key to understanding social relations. Horror is evoked through transgression of boundaries, including bodily boundaries. In these films, the body is no longer bounded, but porous and open to infiltration. J-Horror, as with Western horror, is based on the breaching of space. Bodily breaches in J-Horror occur in a number of ways: through death by curse and transposition and disruption of representation (e.g., photographs and bodily mutilation).

Understanding transgression of boundaries is paramount to understanding horror. A lack of clear boundaries signals confusion and disorder. Where there is disorder, there is often an impulse to rectify it and to institute order and control. This occurs when public and private spaces overlap or with any boundary violation. The fear of transgression can be applied to the body as well. For instance, the penetrated and transgressed body is disturbing because it doesn't uphold boundaries between interior and exterior. It becomes porous and fluid. Cultural theorist Mary Douglas argues that "all margins are dangerous. If they are pulled this way or that the shape of fundamental experience is altered."[15] There is an anxiety in society about the porous and liminal characteristics of the body.

The liminal body inhabits the line between spaces and, as such, occupies both spaces at the same time while not fully occupying either. This is where horror occurs. It occurs when and where the body becomes both and neither simultaneously. For instance, the penetrated body plays with understandings of interior and exterior, while the possessed body disturbs notions of Self and Other.

Liminal bodies elide boundaries and disturb categories. When these bodies breach the boundaries between good and evil, interior and exterior, and Self and Other, they show the vulnerability of these socially constructed dualisms. The frailty of these categories is protected in Western horror through punishment (either through death, mutilation, rape, or possession) of those who transgress their borders. In J-Horror, punishment may also happen, but it is not necessarily guaranteed.

Women's bodies, in particular, confuse bodily boundaries due to their capacity to reproduce (menstruation, pregnancy, childbirth). While the female body is one that is portrayed as particularly abject (in regard to menstruation, childbirth, and the like), human bodies, regardless of sex, are abject in that they are not bounded entities. In horror, both male and female bodies become objects of horror because they do not remain bounded. They become liminal spaces. Intrusion is a common event for many horror films. Gillian Beer argues that ghost stories "'elide the distance between the actual and the imagined.' They speak, literally and figuratively, of an intrusion into the everyday world. In ghost stories, 'the fictional takes place in the everyday: it takes space, and . . . the usurpation of space by the immaterial . . . is one of the deepest terrors released by the ghost story . . . [G]host stories are to do with the insurrection, not the resurrection, of the dead.'"[16] Many J-Horror films are ghost stories that use the body as a liminal space. Since the body is the most personal and intimate of spaces, its porous boundary is horrific and unsettling to the viewer. Others may breach the body through acts of violence.

The Films

The films I examine here reveal multiple geographies, which then reflect multiple social relations. Social relations are fluid and contested rather than fixed. There are a number of complex geographies at play in these J-Horror texts.

Cultural and feminist geographies are evidenced by recurring tropes within the J-Horror genre. For instance, the prevalence of dark water in these films symbolizes the fear of tsunamis hitting the island state of Japan. Water has to do with physical geography, but the word "wet" can also mean "emotional" in Japanese. Additionally, it is damp settings rather than dry ones that the Japanese associate with spirits. In Western horror movies, the bathroom is also a frequent backdrop to terror. J-Horror makes audiences recoil by suggesting that a disembodied spirit is about to creep into a damp space, a space so damp that it is hard to breathe. Suicide in these films also reflects rising suicide rates. The symbol of long, dark, and wild hair is also repeated frequently. In feudal Japan, women were expected to have neat, kempt hair. If hair was unruly, it symbolized madness or possession.[17] By understanding the context of these symbols, one understands how bodies and other spaces are constructed.

In *Ringu*, a group of teenagers in Japan dies simultaneously of unknown causes. The commonality in their deaths is a mysterious videotape they watched together. They receive a phone call that states they have seven days to live shortly after watching the video. After Reiko, a reporter, deciphers the connection between the video and their deaths (including the death of her niece), she realizes that she only has seven days to figure out the meaning behind the tape or she too will die. In her investigation of the mysteries of the videotape, much is revealed about a child named Sadako who has paranormal powers. Reiko uncovers that Sadako was murdered due to these supernatural powers and her revenge forms the basis for the deaths of those who watch the haunted video. *Ringu* is not a slasher film, but instead a thriller that mixes modern technology with Japanese folklore (another recurrent theme in J-Horror). *Ringu* was remade and Westernized into the film, *The Ring*. It kick-started J-Horror in American media followed soon by remakes of *The Grudge* (2004) and *Dark Water* (2005).

Dark Water focuses on a woman (abandoned by her mother as a child) and her struggles to raise her own daughter. Yoshimi is involved in a bitter custody battle with her ex-husband over daughter Ikuko. Yoshimi is unemployed and in need of a home. When viewing a derelict apartment in a Tokyo suburb, Yoshimi finds an exploring Ikuko on the roof carrying a red child's bag, which is full of toys. Yoshimi takes the bag from Ikuko and throws it in the garbage, thinking no more of it. The bag reappears shortly after. After they move into the dilapidated apartment, they are soon plagued by water seeping through the ceiling. Along with the water comes the ghost of the child who lived in the apartment above. Yoshimi becomes concerned when she finds Ikuko chattering away to an invisible friend called Mitsuko in their bathroom. Eventually Yoshimi herself begins to see visions of a little girl dressed in yellow around the apartment building and realizes that Ikuko's invisible friend may be a missing child.

One night, Yoshimi finds Ikuko, half-drowned and unconscious, upstairs in the empty apartment above theirs. The apartment had once belonged to Mitsuko's family. After some investigation, Yoshimi discovers that Mitsuko drowned in the apartment building's water tower while trying to retrieve her red bag. While Yoshimi is coming to this conclusion, Ikuko is confronted by Mitsuko's spirit who attempts to drown her in order to take her place as daughter. Yoshimi finds Ikuko unconscious on the bathroom floor. Yoshimi picks up Ikuko and races to the elevator to flee the apartment. But as the elevator door closes, she realizes the girl in her arms is Mitsuko, who claims Yoshimi as mother. Yoshimi eventually saves her daughter and protects her from Mitsuko's ghost by giving herself to Mitsuko as a substitute mother figure for the one she lost. The film ends with Ikuko, now sixteen, realizing that her mother's spirit has been watching over her all along as she grows up.

Audition, a cult film not reworked into a Western version, follows the story of a man and his search for love. Seven years after the death of his wife, widower Aoyama decides to remarry. At the urging of his friend, he holds a fake movie-casting session to "audition" potential brides, unbeknownst to the women. One application, that of Asami, contains the statement: "Live or die, it's just a thin line between them." These words will come to have deeper meaning as the film progresses. Aoyama chooses Asami, a former ballet dancer, and begins a serious relationship with her. During a romantic weekend, she disappears after she asks Aoyama to love her and only her. As Aoyama attempts to find out what has happened to Asami, he discovers a dark past that includes abuse by her uncle and suggestions of murder and abduction. Asami returns and gruesomely attacks Aoyama because he has betrayed her by not fulfilling his promise to love her alone (Aoyama was having multiple affairs with his secretary and his son's girlfriend). The climax of the film has Asami clothed in a PVC apron and gloves outfitted with acupuncture needles and wire saw exacting her revenge.

The Grudge is a remake of the Japanese film *Ju-On*. The film jumps in time, although the setting remains the same. While two sequels followed, only *The Grudge* is analyzed here. The Grudge is a curse born when one dies in the grip of a powerful rage or sorrow. The curse manifests at the time of death.

The film follows the Saeki family (past timeline) as well as a woman named Karen Davis (present timeline). Kayako Saeki is murdered by her husband, Taeko, in a jealous rage when he believes she is unfaithful to him with her professor. Losing his mind, he also kills his son and the family's cat. After Taeko hides the bodies, he is murdered by Kayako's spirit (appearing as a pale figure in a white kimono with long, dark, unkempt hair). The professor comes to the house and commits suicide after finding Kayoko's body as the curse begins.

When the American Williams family moves into the house, Matt and Jennifer are killed by the Grudge (in the form of Toshio) leaving behind Matt's mother, Emma. The older woman needs nurse's care and Karen Davis is hired after the original caretaker goes missing.

Kayako begins to haunt Karen, and Karen, with the help of a detective, investigates the house and its prior tenants. After learning of the murders, the detective tries to burn the house down, but is killed by the curse. When Karen realizes her boyfriend has gone to look for her in the house, she finds him paralyzed with fear at the site of Kayako and he dies of fright. Karen then attempts to torch the house, but the house survives, as does Karen. Unfortunately, Karen is still haunted by Kayako as the film ends.

Liminal Spaces I: The Body

The body in these films is a contested space. It often becomes a space that is two things at one time. It is a liminal space, open to the paranormal. For example, in *Ringu*, photos of the victims show smudged, almost ghostly faces. This not only shows those who have been marked, but illuminates another moment of liminality—they may still be alive, but they are cursed and soon on the path to death.

In *Ringu*, Sadako is the most liminal of characters. She represents the space between worlds. Sadako, in the original story behind *Ringu*, is a hermaphrodite embodying the liminal space between male and female. She is history, present, and the future intertwined. She is a body trapped between good and evil. She is the monster who was victimized. Her body forms a link between the living and dead and her mind between the physical world and the supernatural.

Sadako, left to die in a well, is able to transgress the well into which she was dumped and capture her fury onto a video telepathically cursing those who watch it to die seven days after the viewing. She is able to break the boundaries of the well psychically. The only "cure" for Sadako's curse is to make a copy of the video and pass it on. To survive is to doom another. The curse can be transferred from one body to another, creating a chain of death that links one body to another in a paranormal manner.

In one pivotal scene, Reiko's ex-husband is watching Sadako's video.

While he is watching the video, Sadako breaches the television and becomes a physical form. Sadako's body is drenched, saturated with well water. She walks in a jilted way and is characterized by pale skin and long, black hair that covers her face. Her fingernails are missing from trying to claw her way out of the well. When she emerges from the reel world television into the real world, she transgresses yet another boundary. Other liminal moments happen when Yoichi, Reiko's young son, feels the presence of his deceased cousin in her room. Yoichi also feels a strong connection to Sadako.

In *Dark Water*, bodily spaces are transgressed by all three of the key characters: Yoshimi, Ikuko, and Mitsuko. The border of the world between living and dead is held in very delicate tension throughout the movie. Odd events plague Yoshimi (and Ikuko). No matter how many times Yoshimi disposes of Mitsuko's red bag, it reappears in various places. Mitsuko is able to breach the bounds of her afterlife in multiple ways. Her long, dark hair is found in running tap water. Yoshimi continually catches a glimpse of a young, long-haired girl, which breaches the boundary between living/dead and sanity/insanity, for Yoshimi feels as though she is seeing things that are not truly there. When Yoshimi finds a nearly drowned Ikuko in the apartment upstairs, the walls are streaming with water that floods the apartment. Yoshimi wants to move (thinking that something supernatural is happening), but her lawyer convinces her that her eyes may be deceiving her and that moving could hurt her custody case.

In the film's climactic scene, Mitsuko replaces Ikuko in Yoshimi's arms. Mitsuko is able to physically take Ikuko's place. The boundaries between their young bodies are fluid. The border between life and death is evidenced by Yoshimi's decision to leave the living Ikuko and protect her by succumbing to the wishes of the dead girl. She is mother in both life and death.

Dark Water ends with Ikuko at the age of sixteen revisiting her once home. The old apartment looks surprisingly well kept. She then sees her mother, Yoshimi. Her mother states that when Ikuko is happy, she too is happy. Ikuko then asks if she can stay with her mother, believing her to still be alive. Yoshimi tells her that would be impossible. Sensing something, Ikuko turns around, but sees nothing (although Mitsuko is briefly on screen). When she turns back, Yoshimi is gone. Here we see that death cannot keep Yoshimi from Ikuko and that death is overcome so that Yoshimi can watch over Ikuko. Although her body has been claimed by the spirit world, Yoshimi has a view onto the physical world in order to see her daughter.

Audition is a film primarily based in the physical world. Its horror is based on bodily torture and mutilation. In several scenes, bodies are either dismembered or in the process of mutilation. One scene in particular is that of nightmares. In Asami's apartment, we see a large sack. When the sack first twitches, the line between animate and inanimate is crossed. In a frightening reveal, the sack contains a man missing three fingers, his tongue, and an ear, which links back to an earlier scene—the discovery of the dismembered body of Asami's boss. When he was reassembled, he was found to have three fingers, a tongue, and an ear too many. The feet of the man in the sack have also been cut off. When he crawls out of the sack and begs for food, Asami vomits into a dog dish and places it in front of him. The man then sticks his face in the bowl of vomit and consumes it. The inside of the body becomes outside when Asami vomits and then the outside becomes the inside when the man ingests that same vomit.

Other instances that depict transgression of bodily boundaries include the burning of Asami's legs by her uncle and, of course, the climactic torture scene. In this scene, Asami drugs Aoyama's whiskey and then injects a second paralytic into his tongue. She states that the body is paralyzed, but the "nerves are awake." She then cuts off his foot with a wire saw. In this scene of mutilation, Asami says: "Kiri-kiri-kiri" (deeper-deeper-deeper) and digs into the boundary of the body breaching exterior boundaries and cutting into the interior. While she is in process of cutting off the other foot, Aoyama's son comes home and kills her. Although the film's ending may be allegorical as Asami's guilt may be concocted by Aoyama as a way to assuage his guilt of not being able to remain faithful to her, it still evokes a strong, visceral response by the viewer.

Liminal Spaces II: The Home

While most of the examples used here are about the body as a liminal and transgressive space, the home can also be a space of horror. When home boundaries break down, traditional ideologies regarding the home can be challenged. Vivian Sobchack posits that with this breakdown, a man's home ceases to be his patriarchal castle due to the "invasive presence of Others."[18] When the Other breaches the home, it opens up the previously private domain and makes it public. Sobchack continues this argument by stating that the Other can "become part of the family, and open up the kitchen and family room up to the horrific and wondrous world outside this private and safe domain."[19] Transgressed spatial boundaries evoke horror. When the Others are removed from the home, the film concludes. Those who invade the home by transgressing the public-private divide are punished and this punishment reinforces gendered codings of space.[20]

This horrific blur of the public and private draws on dominant assumptions of those spaces in order to evoke feelings of terror. When the home becomes fluid and spatial boundaries break down, the myth is exposed that there is a "distinction between family members and alien Others, between private home and public space, between personal microcosm and sociopolitical macrocosm."[21]

Much as we see the home as a site of invasion in *Dark Water*, the home becomes a conduit for ghosts in *The Grudge*. *The Grudge* is a classic haunted-house story with a twist. Characters that enter the house are cursed. The normal façade of a modest house in Tokyo belies the hidden terror within. It is possessed by a violent plague that destroys the lives of everyone who enters. Known as "the Grudge," this curse causes its victims to die in the grip of a powerful rage. Those who are fatally afflicted by the curse die and a new curse is born—it is passed like a virus to all those who enter the house in an endless, growing chain of horror. Within this house, the terror has been set in motion by a terrifying evil that was born years before. As more people die, protagonist Karen is pulled into the cycle of horror and learns the secret of the vengeful curse that has taken root in this house.

The Grudge also tells the tale of the murder of housewife Kayako by her jealous husband. He was enraged when he discovered her secret love for a college professor after reading her diary. Clad in a white kimono, a traditional Japanese outfit for the dead, Kayako returns as a vengeful ghost and starts killing those who enter her house by literally scaring them to death. Takashi Shimizu, the director of *The Grudge*, stated in an interview, "From ancient times, and historically speaking, Japanese women have always been told to stay inside the house and walk one step behind their husband."[22] He additionally pointed out that *okusan*, a Japanese word for a wife, literally means "inside person."[23] Shimizu observed: "Women had been long confined by their husbands and society and their anger and frustration had been bottled up inside. I am drawn to their deep grudge and female tenacity. For me, American zombies and serial murderers are so dry. They don't reflect deep ill-feelings. But in Japanese horror, just watching a ghost scares me because I can feel its tenacious grudge."[24]

Geographies of J-Horror

These horror texts show the liminal and transgressed body as a terrifying place, playing into fears regarding the borders of both the body and home. The bodies in *Ringu*, *Dark Water*, and *Audition* are represented as in-between spaces and sites of conflict, while the private space of the home is represented as a space of assault in *The Grudge*. These portrayals contribute to both the strengthening and the undermining of hegemonic narratives of the body and home.

Horror evokes the most basic of instincts. Often a viewer of a horror film feels not only a psychological reaction, but also a visceral one. These fears are based on transgressions of boundaries and liminal spaces. As geographers well know, boundaries are continually constructed, challenged, and redefined. In the horror texts considered here, the divides between the living and the dead and interior and exterior are porous and disconcerting. The body and home become conduits within these horror stories, permeable to the outside. They are no longer isolated and segregated; they are invaded.

The breaching of the reel world into the real world creates unease and fear. The reel/real world binary breaks down within these J-Horror texts, especially in *Ringu* and *Audition* as they involve explicit interplay between the reel and the real (e.g., *Audition* holds a fake movie casting and *Ringu* involves the breaching of space through the viewing of the video). These two instances show how movies tease the line between both sides of the dualism. This tension can lead to feelings of anxiety in the audience.

In exploring these films, we revisit virtual affectivity and how it influences not only the viewer, but the process of public privates. The corporeal experience of these films is both embodied and disembodied. Some characters have corporeality; others—such as a ghost—do not. The elision that happens between public and private spaces provokes horror and feelings of visceral abjection. It projects a sense of unease that disturbs the viewer.

4

Visions of Gender

Codings of Televisual Space

Television is a popular and powerful medium that reaches into billions of homes across the world every day. In front of their televisions, people eat, perform various tasks, or simply relax. In the past decade, technological advances have changed the way that many watch television. With the advent of mobile device viewing, viewers are no longer bound to their couches; nor are they tied to a programming schedule because DVRs, on-demand services, and streaming websites such as Hulu, Netflix, and Amazon Prime have freed them from fixed viewing windows. No matter when or where one watches, there is a relationship between the viewer and the viewed. Interactions between audience and television form gendered identities. Television—through its depiction of everyday life in the workplace, the home, and third spaces—creates gendered codings of space. This chapter seeks to spotlight the role that television plays in forming gendered socio-spatial relations of (re)production by showing how several classic popular sitcoms, set in both the workplace and in the home, reinforce traditional patriarchal frameworks.

I use the term "(re)production" to designate moments of both production and reproduction. It can be used to explore production, as in the creation of television, and reproduction, as in the multiplication of this effect. It serves as shorthand as well. By production, I simply mean waged labor, whereas reproduction is composed of activities that support waged labor (such as childcare, housework, and cooking). Reproduction is traditionally coded as female and associated with private space and the home.[1] Production is seen as male and linked to public space and the workplace. Domestic labor within the private sphere is considered to be reproduction and is valued less than production (the labor that is traditionally considered to take place within the public sphere).[2] Feminist geographers have undermined and transformed the hegemony that views reproduction as inferior to production. The dualisms of public/private and production/reproduction are subverted when reproduction is linked to production through an interdependent relationship. When domestic/reproductive labor is seen as key to the revitalization of the production worker and therefore essential to the production process, the hierarchy of production over reproduction is challenged. By taking such a stance, reproductive labor can be redefined as productive by referring to it as the reproduction of labor power.[3] This definition destabilizes the hierarchy and provides reproductive labor with a legitimate and intrinsic role in the production process.

Interconnection between social relations and time can be used to define space: actions occur in space and time and they create/define space and time.[4] This definition of space is not complete though, because it does not explore power relations. Doreen Massey uses these power relations in a further definition of space in which space is a dynamic net of dominant and subordinate relations.[5]

In Gillian Rose's *Feminism and Geography*, she argues that feminist geographers need to be concerned with the public/private and production/reproduction dualisms.[6] Rose discusses how patriarchal power relations define gendered spaces and gender identities. Rose also discusses how the relations of production create different codes of spaces (e.g., the private as reproductive and the public as productive). Rose posits that the power relations that define space show the unequal relations between the sexes and vice versa.

Unequal relations between the sexes are mapped out in space as women are associated with private/reproductive spaces and reproductive labor is judged to be of lesser value than productive labor. Women are traditionally linked to private space due to their performance of reproductive duties such as the upkeep of the home and the caretaking of children. This reproductive work is valued as inferior due to the lack of paid wages. The link between women and private space has been naturalized over time.[7] This could be due in part to the fact that the relationship between women and the reproductive role is sometimes given a biological spin—that women are naturally better nurturers due to their birthing capabilities.[8]

Another aspect of private space is the notion that "a man's home is his castle." This links the masculine to private space in a much different relationship than the feminine relationship to the home. It provides the masculine with patriarchal autonomy and places the feminine in an inferior role.[9] Work within the home is not valued because it is traditionally unpaid labor. Patriarchy and capitalism are spatialized due to this relation to private/public spaces.

In the Western world, public space has long been defined as masculine due to the large role that men have had in the production process for centuries. Until only a few decades ago, men were usually the only members of the family to work outside the home. Women—if they participated in wage labor—worked out of the home in cottage industries or through various forms of subcontracting. Patriarchal definitions of spaces by society as masculine or feminine affect individual perceptions of space and identity. This link between gender identity, patriarchy, and space is a cultural phenomenon, and in recent history there has been no greater influence on popular culture than television.

Stereotypes portrayed on television reinforce gendered social relations of (re)production. Television creates idealized images that influence identity and gender roles within the audience. These roles play out in both the public and private domains depending on the sitcom setting. Gendered ideals form gendered spaces—both on the television screen and within reality—through the portrayal and legitimization of gendered social relations of (re)production.

Drawing from feminist theorizations of the reciprocal relations between gendered spaces and the constitution of gendered identities and relations, this chapter problematizes the gendered spaces television constructs. I highlight examples from television sitcoms to show how television reinforces the hierarchies of public/private and production/reproduction. The danger of these images and the reinforcement of the patriarchal hierarchies can be seen in how television manifests gendered codings of public and private spaces. When these become legitimized, they can be utilized in forming public law, policy, and behaviors.[10] Regardless of universal acceptance, their very presence gives them the right to influence social and political institutions. Television can oppress by reinforcing dominant audience ideologies.[11]

Images emitted from the television screen influence both public and private spaces. By showing images that reinforce traditional gendered codings, television participates in and services patriarchy. Television helps to legitimize gender relations that affect the audience and framings of public and private spaces through the repetitive portrayal of traditional and patriarchal gender roles. Portrayals of productive and reproductive labor as unequal and gendered and how these portrayals lead to gendered spaces within the public and private spheres are areas that need to be addressed further by feminist and cultural geographers due to the effect that television has on constructing codings of gendered spaces.

Contradictions that subvert patriarchy also occur in every show discussed for this chapter. For instance, in *The Cosby Show*, the mother character of Clair Huxtable is a successful lawyer with five children. Her husband, Dr. Cliff Huxtable, is an obstetrician-gynecologist whose office is within the family home. This setup for a show seems contrary to the traditional notion of the home as a feminized place, but other aspects of the show reinforce the feminization of reproduction, and thus, the home.

Another example of destabilization and simultaneous reinforcement occurs in *The Mary Tyler Moore Show*, which was considered revolutionary by many feminists due to the focus on an unmarried woman interested in a career, not simply a job. Within this show, Mary's relationships with her coworkers (especially her boss, Lou Grant) undermine the groundbreaking potential of the premise. Although the show is set in a workplace, Mary adopts familial roles with her colleagues. To most of her coworkers, she is a mother figure, while Lou assumes a fatherly role and treats Mary as a daughter.

The examination of the televisual construction of identities by feminist geographers has placed a critical lens on the interaction between the television and the audience.[12] Yet the connection between television's construction of identity and gendered social relations of (re)production has not often been addressed. While Rose concentrates on gender identity in her discussion of soap operas, she focuses on the reinforcing effect these television shows have on stereotypes of women.[13] Rose does not discuss the possibilities for contradictions and paradoxes within soap operas nor does she provide discussion of how these soap operas affect the private realm. Rose keeps the discussion brief and at the spatial level of community. Other prominent works on feminist televisual analysis include the second edition of Charlotte Brunsdon and Lynn Spigels's *Feminist Television Criticism: A Reader*.[14] This edited collection focuses on sitcoms, soap operas, talk shows, and the like to provide a feminist critique of television. While works on the gendered coding of television exist, there is still a dearth of geographical literature on this subject.

An important area of study in feminist geography is the construction of public and private spaces in which production and reproduction take place, traditionally in that order, and the role of such spaces in constituting gender ideologies and relations. Feminist geography needs to focus more attention on the effects that television has on gender identities and codings of space, namely public and private spaces. Television can revolutionize gender relations or it can continue to reinforce existing patriarchal structures. In many cases—although television has helped to bring feminist issues to the forefront—it still retains a patriarchal structure in its construction of gender roles and identities.

According to Bonnie Dow, television sitcoms are the "type of programming in which women are most often and most centrally represented and from which television's most resonant feminist representations have emerged."[15] Of the 427 sitcoms (from 1947 to 1990) Julie D'Acci studied for her work on sitcoms, 256 had women as lead characters.[16] Out of these 256 shows, several strong feminist characters have appeared and brought feminist issues to the forefront. One of the most notable characters is that of Maude from the 1970s sitcom *Maude*. Maude brought feminist issues such as abortion into the living room when she chose at age forty-seven to have an abortion.[17] Over forty years later, this issue is still considered taboo for television (see "Navigating *Degrassi*" in this volume). Other examples include single women as career women (*The Mary Tyler Moore Show*); mothers working outside the home (*Roseanne*, *The Cosby Show*); and single mothers (*Murphy Brown*). These classic sitcoms were progressive in their portrayals both of feminist issues and the changing roles of women and their dynamic families.

If television can help to change gender relations, then it can also change the coding and gendering of spaces and subvert traditional hierarchical notions of public and private spaces and, therefore, (re)production. Gender identity is closely linked to space and the construction of that space. Sophie Bowlby, Jo Foord, and Linda McDowell argue that gendered identity in public and private spaces are contingent upon changing social and historical relations in the home, workplace, and community.[18] It is that link between social and historical relations in space that has led to the gendered coding of spaces and the gendering of social relations of (re)production. The dichotomies of public/private and production/reproduction are closely tied to gender identity because they often provide patriarchal guides to what it means to be a man or a woman. Gendered social relations in the home, workplace, and community can be partially formed by television.

Gendered Constructions of Space within TV Sitcoms

Television continually reinforces the framework that there are gender roles to follow through the portrayal of characters, their interaction with others, and the activities they perform in the spaces they occupy. Within these classic sitcoms, there is a formula for how men and women should act within public and private spaces. Humor comes many times when characters deviate from these socially constructed and gendered formulae.

It is useful to examine some of the most popular twentieth-century television sitcoms, including *Roseanne*, *The Cosby Show*, *The Mary Tyler Moore Show*, and *Murphy Brown*, according to their portrayal of characters in public and private spaces. Analysis consists of showing how these television sitcoms created images of and ideals for what a Mother, Father, or Working Woman should be as well as the spatial constructions of the home and workplace.

These shows were chosen for investigation due to their popularity, long runs, and the content of each series. The historical times in which these programs aired were also considered so that shows from different periods in the television era were examined. Due to syndication, all of these shows can currently be seen by television viewers and continue to have an influence on the construction of gendered spaces and gender identity. Although they are distinct in themselves, they will be used to show some general trends within sitcoms, namely the spatial constructions of gender identity within the home and workplace. These television shows still influence today's society in the proliferation of reruns and from the identities and social relations they constructed in decades past. It should also be recognized that the audience has an influence on the programs they watch and that the construction of gendered identities and social relations of (re)production is not a simple unilinear process and not fully understood.

Each of the sitcoms constructs gendered spaces. The home is represented as a feminized space due to the continual representation of a gendered division of labor within the home. Yet in many cases, it is also constructed as the stereotypical male refuge. The performance of domestic responsibilities by women in the family, not men, continually reinforces "a man's home is his castle" motif. Similar to the home as a complex place, the workplace is also portrayed as a contradictory space in the workplaces of sitcoms. There are both feminist and masculinist constructions in each setting.

The images, spaces, and relations that these sitcoms create come through the use and reinforcement of traditional hierarchies regarding public/private and production/reproduction. Once again, it should be stated that each television program contains contradictory elements that undermine the traditional patriarchal frameworks that value the public over the private and productive labor over reproductive, but overwhelmingly, these shows reinforce patriarchal hierarchies.

Televisual Constructions of the Home

The home is constructed as a feminized place, even a burden, as well as a masculinized haven through the televisual depiction of mothers and fathers. Television constructs images of the ideal home through its representation of parenthood in various programs. For most audiences, the sitcoms that exemplify traditional notions of a home as a "man's castle" and as the responsibility of the wife/mother are those from the mid-twentieth century, such as *Leave It to Beaver*. There are, of course, many other shows from that era that portray the same picture of a nuclear family.

During this time, traditional and patriarchal images and unrealistic depictions of family life dominated television. Yet during this period in history, women were entering the workforce at unprecedented rates.[19] This conflict between reality and television was virtually ignored by the television industry. The television industry also ignored the fact that in order to reach the economic and material level of these shows, a double income was needed.[20] Representation of mothers staying at home with the children while fathers head off to work is more difficult to find on television today, and televisual women have come a long way since Mrs. Cleaver cooked for her son, the "Beav."[21] Yet the patriarchal foundation that supported and created Mrs. Cleaver can still be found in shows today.

At first glance, the television sitcom *Roseanne* seems to be in direct contradiction with the patriarchy of the 1950s. *Roseanne* fought the ideology of "true" womanhood and constructions of perfect wives and mothers by curating an image of a disobedient woman.[22] In "The Fifties Show," the main character of *Roseanne*, Roseanne Conner, parodies the classic clichés of the midcentury housewife of that decade right down to the pearls. But upon closer examination, *Roseanne* creates a gendered coding of the home and at times broadcasts an image of Mother and Father comparable to those in such sitcoms as *Leave It to Beaver*.

The sitcoms of earlier decades—like *Leave It to Beaver*—idealize family life. They create a picture of domestic harmony with only the occasional mishap to spice up life. The Beaver may lose his new bike to a neighborhood con-artist-in-training, but at the end of the show, all is well. Beaver has his bike back and learns a lesson. Although the episodes of *Roseanne* do not always end with the prototypical happy ending, a matriarchy is portrayed through the enormous amount of power Roseanne Conner wields in the family and within the home.[23]

Roseanne (1988–1997) focuses on the struggles of the Conner family. They are a blue-collar family living paycheck to paycheck and often cannot make ends meet. With multiple mortgages on their house, money is always an issue. Matriarch Roseanne and her husband, Dan, have four children: daughters Becky and Darlene and sons DJ and Jerry. They strive to be more unconventional parents than their own. This is exemplified when they eventually take in David (Darlene's boyfriend and subsequent husband) and Becky's eventual husband, Mark. Mark and David coincidentally are brothers. Jackie, Roseanne's sister, is featured in nearly every episode, but has a subordinate relationship with her older sibling. The series follows the family through several socioeconomic setbacks, including death, depression, divorce, and unemployment. Throughout their journeys, love and humor prevail.

Roseanne Conner is a self-proclaimed "domestic goddess" who definitely wears the metaphorical pants in the family. She is in control of the bills and all reproductive and domestic household duties, she makes decisions about and for the children (even when they are adults), and dominates everyone in her familial and social sphere.

The Conner home is a bungalow set on Delaware Street in Lanford, Illinois. The home is modest and not lavishly decorated. It has a bit of a kitsch factor with decorations such as a painting of dogs playing poker and an afghan blanket thrown over the plaid couch. The recliner is reserved almost exclusively for Dan, and the whole room is focused around the television set.

Characters are often depicted watching the TV. In "Couch Potatoes," the Conners are selected to be a Nielsen Family. They try to change their viewing habits in order to not be seen as "white trash" by the survey. When Dan and Roseanne have a vicious fight over his health in "Fights and Stuff," she destroys the television set, saying, "I'm just trying to do whatever it takes to get you up off of your ass and stop staring at that damn TV!"

The kitchen is another important and popular setting for the show. A large portion of the action of the series takes place there including family dinners, washing dishes, poker games, and more than a few fights. The kitchen floor is linoleum and the brown refrigerator is ever filled with beer and soda. The pantry contains pickled eggs and junk food. Much to Roseanne's chagrin, there is no dishwasher for most of the show's run. The kitchen is attached to a mud porch and the back door leading to the kitchen is a common family entrance.

The prominence of the home in *Roseanne* is key to understanding the coding of space within the show. The tremendous power Roseanne has in the household only shows, in comparison, how little power she typically had in the productive sphere (barring her co-ownership of the Lunch Box diner). Throughout the years, many episodes have focused on her inability to find or keep a job or her dissatisfaction with her job. Roseanne has worked in a myriad of jobs ranging from factory worker to telemarketer to restaurateur (her only successful endeavor). These workplaces will be discussed in more detail below.

Roseanne's initial and continued inability to find success in the productive sphere (until she starts the diner) only ties her closer to the reproductive activities of her home. She often struggles to balance the burdens of home and work. Essentially, she works double duty. Roseanne is the center of her home, she is the glue that holds the family together, and she enjoys her status immensely. Roseanne knows that she is the matriarch within that home and always makes sure that those in her family know that she has the upper hand.

Many times within the domestic setting Roseanne treats her husband, Dan, as an imbecile when it comes to reproductive duties. In the pilot episode "Life and Stuff," she and Dan fight over dinner:

DAN: You want dinner? Fine. I'm fixing dinner!

ROSEANNE: Oh, but honey, you just cooked dinner three years ago!

This exchange serves only to further underscore the patriarchal framework by feminizing the reproductive instead of subverting it. The character of Dan also reinforces this framework by his unwillingness or inability to perform domestic duties. If it is his responsibility to prepare dinner, he orders pizza. If the house needs cleaning before Mom gets home, Dan orders the children to do it, with one exception, in "Workin' Overtime," when Roseanne has extra work responsibilities.

Dan's buffer from the responsibilities of caring for the children or doing housework constructs an image of a father who finds a haven within the home. His main activity within the home is watching television with a beer in his hand. If not in the recliner, he is out in the garage fixing motorcycles. Behind the recliner perched on the mantle are an old football and football trophies. He frequently regales the family and friends with old sports stories. With those images, it can be seen why Dan's home is his "castle."

Dan's interactions with his four children are also an excellent example of how *Roseanne* reinforces patriarchal stereotypes of gender identities. Dan is characterized by stereotypical macho activities. He is a blue-collar worker and a former high school football player; he rides motorcycles, drinks beer, and loves sports. These characteristics define his masculinity and affect his relationships with his children. Of note to this survey of Roseanne is the fact that the character of Dan Conner was ranked number thirteen in TV Guide's list of the "50 Greatest TV Dads of All Time" in the June 20, 2004, issue. However, this "honor" does not change my analysis or argument regarding spaces within the show.

Dan's relationship with his daughter, Darlene, is very involved until she changes from an outgoing tomboy to a young woman more interested in working on a comic book with her boyfriend than shooting hoops or watching the Chicago Bulls on television. Dan becomes frustrated with Darlene as she no longer exhibits masculine traits, and he is confused about how to interact with her. Their relationship deteriorates over time as she grows up and becomes less masculinized. Their relationship both disrupts and reinforces gender norms. Darlene's tomboyishness disrupts gender norms, while the deteriorated relationship reinforces them since Dan is mystified and confused by his daughter as she exhibits feminine traits. Dan is livid when Darlene gets pregnant and chooses to marry David, her boyfriend and father of the baby. He fears that she is "ruining" her life and will not be able to finish college. He sees it as taking a hard road in life at such a young age.

Roseanne, as the social center of the family, coaches Dan on how to interact with his two daughters as they become young women. In one episode, Roseanne is worried about Dan's lack of interaction with his oldest daughter, Becky, who exhibits the most stereotypical feminine traits of the family. In more than one episode, Roseanne tells Dan to go up to Becky and Darlene's room to initiate a conversation with Becky. The conversation is misconstrued as a meddling attempt by Becky and ends in an argument.

Dan turns to Roseanne time and again for advice on his relationship with Becky. Dan's relationship with Becky is never strong and, at one point, is severed when she elopes after Dan's motorcycle shop closes. Dan is bewildered by his daughters and can never quite figure out how to talk to them unless Roseanne guides him.

Dan's relationship with his oldest son is also strained. DJ is a boy more interested in movies than sports. His football-playing, motorcycle-loving father is bewildered by the lack of "masculine" traits in his son. In one episode, Dan sets out to strengthen his relationship with DJ. He grabs an old football off the shelf and pulls DJ out the door to play football while DJ complains, "Do I have to?" When DJ is bullied in "Punch and Jimmy," Dan is disgusted to find out that DJ would rather fall into the fetal position than defend himself by fighting. Dan is further disgraced and upset by DJ's actions when he finds out the bully is a girl. Dan is only able to really relate to DJ over puberty.

Roseanne "allows" Dan to take charge of the situation when DJ handles unwanted erections in school by playing dumb in "The Parenting Trap."

DAN: Okay, I'll talk to him.
ROSEANNE: Well, that's great, 'cause I know you'll do a great job.

DAN: Yeah?

ROSEANNE: Yeah.

DAN: You mean it?

ROSEANNE: Yeah. Hey, I've got an idea. Why don't you bounce off me what you're gonna say to DJ? You know I'm sure it will be fine, and everything, but maybe this way, I could learn something, okay? Okay, I'll be DJ.

DAN: Okay. Well, Deej, uh, being a student is really important because someday soon, you're gonna be out in the real world, and you're gonna wanna be smart enough to know when you're getting hosed by your wife.

Dan teaches him to "put a book in front of it," but Roseanne meddles in this situation as well, telling DJ a story about her menarche that he finds traumatizing. DJ runs screaming from the room. Dan confronts Roseanne:

DAN: Say it. I handled the situation better than you.

ROSEANNE: Fine, Dan. You handled it better than me. Happy now?

DAN: If I were any happier, I'd need a book.

A few more examples of conflict between parenting styles occur in the series. When Roseanne allows Darlene to go to a concert out of town in "Good Girls, Bad Girls," Dan is angered by her decision and confronts his wife when Darlene is still not home in the wee hours of the night:

DAN: You said let her go.

ROSEANNE: I said don't.

DAN: She could be out there, god knows where. This never would've happened if you listened to me. Kids shouldn't go to no rock concert.

ROSEANNE: Only middle-aged couples should go.

DAN: You're not off the hook for this. You let her do whatever the hell she wants. This time . . . I don't even want to think about this time.

ROSEANNE: So go ahead and say it. Go on, just say it—I'm a lousy mother. There. You feel better? Maybe something will happen to her and you can be king, right?

[Darlene then walks in the front door]

These scenes are two examples of the very few situations in the program in which Dan is invested in Roseanne's parenting and its outcome and in which Dan argues that he is correct in his parenting decisions. Overwhelmingly, decisions regarding the children are left to Roseanne. In "Crime and Punishment," Dan sees the principal of DJ's school when DJ is found with "obscene" material. Both the school secretary and the principal state they thought Dan was "dead" and that "Mrs. Conner was a widow" due to his absence from the school and parental duties there.

The only extended period when Roseanne struggles as a parent and can empathize with Dan is during Darlene's depression when she enters high school. Darlene withdraws from the family into her room and books. No one knows how to deal with Darlene or her depression and it creates stress for the Conner family.

Dan's lack of parental authority also manifests in other relationships. Darlene's boyfriend, David, moves in and his bond with Dan is also less than ideal. Dan responds much more positively to Mark, David's brother and Becky's husband, than he does to the artsy David. David often exhibits more feminized traits than Darlene, as evidenced in "The Birds and the Frozen Bees." Dan is irritated with David in "The Thrilla Near the Vanilla Extract" because he criticizes his brother, Mark. Dan reprimands him: "You work part-time at a pizza parlor and spend the rest of your life making ironic comments about everybody else. Irony is for people who don't do anything."

The character of Dan constructs an image of a father that has difficulty relating to his children. He detaches from their lives when they deviate from his ideal of them. Dan prefers, as does Roseanne, to let his wife take care of the family affairs while he sits back and occupies himself with other activities of a more constructed masculine nature (watching sports, fixing motorcycles, drinking beer).

This, once again, sets up Roseanne as a mother who knows her children better than her male counterpart does. This ends up naturalizing her role as a superior caregiver. In "Thanksgiving 1994" and "Maybe Baby," Roseanne and Dan receive some disturbing news about her pregnancy and tensions run high between the couple. They discuss the possibility of terminating the pregnancy.

ROSEANNE: You know, I always thought I could have an abortion, but now I just, I don't think I can. Part of me would always wonder what the kid was going to turn out to be.

Roseanne mistakenly believes that Dan is pressuring her to terminate if a serious medical issue is happening.

DAN: I thought we decided that if there was a serious problem that we would deal with it. We talked about this.
ROSEANNE: Yeah, but everything's different now.
DAN: Why?
ROSEANNE: Because I'm pregnant.
DAN: So you're saying you want to have this baby, no matter what?
ROSEANNE: No, I'm just saying this is a much more complicated situation than I ever thought it would be.

In "Another Mouth to Shut Up," Darlene announces her pregnancy. Roseanne then asks her if she has considered all of her options.

ROSEANNE: Have you considered all the options open to you, you know, having to do with the pregnancy and everything?
DARLENE: Yeah, I . . . I know the options. And I want the baby. I want it more than I've ever wanted anything. Is that so hard to believe?

These two scenes, while different in tone, show the relationship that forms between mother and child, even in utero. Roseanne naturalizes the maternal influence and bond by portraying feelings of motherhood as expected with pregnancy, although there are times when that maternal attachment is not present.

The connection between mother/child/reproduction is a popular tool in constructing the role of Mother. This connection is often used to contrast Mother and Father. *Roseanne* uses the contrast of Roseanne against Dan to construct the idea of Mother through opposition. Roseanne is in opposition to Dan due to her direct involvement with the children. Roseanne always knows what is happening in their lives, or, if she does not, she finds out quickly. Roseanne is portrayed as having knowledge about children that those who have not been mothers (including men and childless women) could not possibly understand or comprehend. In "Let Them Eat Junk," Jackie (Roseanne's sister) leaves her only child in the care of Roseanne with a long list of instructions. The list includes instructions not to feed Andy, the child, any sugar. When Jackie returns, she discovers that Roseanne has fed the child cookies. Jackie is livid with Roseanne. Roseanne's counter to Jackie's ranting is that she has raised three children while Jackie is a new mother who does not know anything yet.

Another example showing the construction of Mother as superior care-giver comes from the presence of the extended family within the household. Roseanne acts as a mother figure to her younger sister, Jackie, allowing her to come over and use the laundry facilities at will or stay with them when she is having problems in her life or feeling ill. Much to the chagrin of Dan, Jackie is not the only family member Roseanne allows to stay in the house. Roseanne took in Darlene's boyfriend, David, when he was having problems with his own mother. After Becky married, Roseanne encourages Becky and her husband, Mark, to move back into the house. This pattern repeats itself in later episodes when Darlene and David (eventually married) move into the house with their new baby.

The home once again here is ruled by the wishes of Roseanne. She decides who lives at the home, her home. When David is thrown out of the house after it is discovered by Dan that he was living with Darlene in Chicago, Roseanne cajoles Dan to bring David back into the home. The Conner home is essentially the space that she dominates.

The character of Roseanne Conner is, in essence, what Rose calls a fantasized maternal Woman.[24] The prevalence of Roseanne's maternal actions and characteristics within the context of the sitcom reinforces the patriarchal ideology that women are dominated by their ability to bear children.[25] Speaking from Rose's framework, this assumption eventually ties Woman back to the home due to construction of Woman as Other to Man. The framework of Woman as (m)Other eventually leads to a mystification of Woman due to her intangibility. Within that framework, (m)Other becomes the heart of the house, family, and home and is tied (by the apron strings, perhaps?) to the private sphere and reproductive work solely on the construction and definition of what it means to be Woman/Mother.[26]

In the closing monologue for the series, Roseanne muses over her life and her chronicling of it in a book she has written:

ROSEANNE: My mom came from a generation where women were supposed to be submissive about everything. I never bought into that, and I wish mom hadn't either. I wish she had made a different choice. When Becky brought David home a few years ago I thought, "This is wrong!" He was much more Darlene's type. When Darlene met Mark, I thought he went better with Becky. I guess I was wrong. But I still think they'd be more compatible the other way around. So in my writing, I did what any good mother would do. I fixed it. . . . Dan and I always felt that it was our responsibility as parents to improve the lives of our children by fifty percent over our own. And we did. We didn't hit our children as we were hit, we didn't demand their unquestioning silence, and we didn't teach our daughters to sacrifice more than our sons. As a modern wife, I walked a tightrope between tradition and progress, and usually, I failed, by one outsider's standards or another's. But I figured out that neither winning nor losing count for women like they do for men. . . . When you're a blue-collar woman and your husband dies it takes away your whole sense of security. . . . For a while I lost myself in food and a depression so deep that I couldn't even get out of bed till I saw that my family needed me to pull through so that they could pull through. . . . And then Darlene had the baby, and it almost died. I snapped out of the mourning immediately, and all of my life energy turned into choosing life.

The relationship that Roseanne has to her family and her home demonstrates the connection between motherhood burdens and private space. It additionally shows how fatherhood excuses Dan from the double duty of his wife. The juxtaposition of the constructions of Mother and Father in the home depicts the patriarchal roles that are both reified and subverted within the show.

Other television sitcoms provide a different construction of Father, but these television shows also help to serve patriarchy. In *The Cosby Show* (1984–92), Cliff Huxtable is a successful obstetrician-gynecologist with his office located in his home. Since his work is located within the domestic sphere, in this sense, the home cannot be simply constructed as a haven for him. But the character of Cliff is constructed in a patriarchal manner, nonetheless. He is an idealized father, an authority figure with a halo. In the 1980s, most of my friends wanted Bill Cosby/Cliff Huxtable as their father. "Cliff Huxtable" was ranked as the best TV dad in the aforementioned June 20, 2004, TV Guide's list of the "50 Greatest TV Dads of All Time." *The Cosby Show* highlights the antics of the Huxtable family: daughters Sondra, Denise, Vanessa, Rudy, and son Theo. The program revitalized the sitcom format in the 1980s.

Cliff Huxtable treats all domestic situations with humor even though he may not always know what is going on with them. For example, Cliff lets one of his daughters, Vanessa, go to an older friend's party. Little does he know that his wife, Clair, has expressly forbidden Vanessa to go. Vanessa preys upon her father's ignorance about her personal life and friends in order to attend the party. Clair later scolds Cliff for letting Vanessa leave the house without checking with her first. This example helps to construct Cliff as a father who is involved with his children, but on a somewhat superficial level.

Many televisual constructions of Father come from less obvious sources, including *The Mary Tyler Moore Show* (1970–77). The sitcom follows the career pursuits and social life of single woman Mary Richards. The show was revolutionary in featuring her character. In the pilot, Mary applies for a secretarial position at a television news station, but is instead hired as an associate producer. Episodes focus on equal pay for women, premarital sex, and homosexuality.

Lou Grant, Mary's boss, is a father figure to her.[27] Lou is a paternal figure to Mary in both personal and business-related situations. Mary consistently seeks Lou's approval on decisions, and evokes—according to Dow—a father-child relationship with plots similar to *Father Knows Best* or *Leave It to Beaver*.[28] Whether Mary is seeking advice about a raise or her love life, Lou always has the answer and at the end of most episodes, his fatherly wisdom is reaffirmed.

Another construction of Father in the selected sitcoms is the opposite from that of "father knows best." It comes from the idea that a father is not needed for children. In the sitcom *Murphy Brown* (1988–98), the titular character does not have a paternal presence in her child's life and, in essence, she portrays the image that a father is not needed to raise a child properly. Murphy Brown, a character whose dominant traits are considered masculine (she is loud, pushy, and aggressive), is a single working mother. Murphy's pregnancy announcement created quite a stir in the real world when then vice president Dan Quayle blasted the character for not portraying "family values," showing how the patriarchal constructed image of Mother is ingrained into society. The "absent father" motif only lends more support to the patriarchal link between mother/child/reproduction.

A superficial glance at the show would seem to refute the naturalization of Murphy as Mother or the mystically maternal Woman. She does not raise her child on her own; she instead has a nanny. As for other connections to domestic duties, Murphy's idea of cooking is to order take-out. But a closer examination of Murphy's interaction with her son, Avery, does lead to a naturalization of Murphy as Mother. Murphy sings to her child "You Make Me Feel Like a Natural Woman."[29] Murphy's masculinity in the workplace, but femininity as a mother, only serves to reinforce the naturalization of women as mothers. If someone as masculine and seemingly nonmaternal as Murphy is made complete by a child, then surely the average female (naturally) would feel the same way. This idea is further exemplified when Murphy coos to Avery, "You're all I need to get by."

Clair Huxtable of *The Cosby Show* is a lawyer with five children. Although it is her husband that works in the home, Clair is linked to private space through her construction as Mother within the show. Clair is much more in touch with her children and their lives than is her husband, although he is present in the home more than she. It would seem logical that Cliff would have more information about the children due to his close proximity to them within the home, but indeed, it is Clair who is the more knowledgeable about their children. This is shown when the children continually come to Clair for personal and private issues, whether it be advice about motherhood or worries about a changing body, rather than Cliff. In "Same Time Next Year," Rudy (the youngest daughter) is concerned about her lack of breasts. After insisting that she wants to speak with her mother about this issue, she is finally coaxed by Cliff to talk about what is bothering her. When Rudy tells Cliff her concerns, he is confused as to why she would speak to her mother, rather than him, her gynecologist father.

Spatial Constructions of the Workplace

Television constructs a gendered workplace in much the same way as it constructs a gendered home. These constructions differ, but also parallel each other. The similarities are the use of patriarchal notions of gendered social relations of (re)production and traditional gender roles for the spatial constructions. These patriarchal notions reinforce the public/private and production/reproduction dichotomies, linking the feminine to the private and reproductive spheres and the masculine to the public and productive spheres. Just as with the constructions of the roles of Mother and Father, the construction of Working Woman tends to support, rather than subvert, the gendered coding of spaces and gender social relations of (re)production.

In the series *Roseanne*, there are a number of workplaces to discuss. She worked at Wellman Plastics, a factory job, for the first season of the show. A job at which—according to a storyline of the show—she had worked for over a decade. She and her closest friends quit when a degrading boss ups their quotas to an unreasonable level. The factory setting is central to understanding gendered roles of production. The factory is populated overwhelmingly with "unskilled" women workers. The workers stand on their feet all day and the work is repetitive. While a secure job with benefits, the wages are low. A dual income is needed for the Conner family to pay bills.

After a period of unemployment, Roseanne starts working from home at a telemarketing magazine sales job. Her family constantly disrupts her job and the blurring of the lines between productive and reproductive labor is noticeable. Roseanne's telemarketing job is a good example of how public privates are manifested within the show and to the viewers.

Roseanne goes on to find work at a beauty salon. While she enjoys her work and her female coworkers, she finds sweeping up hair and shampooing clients demeaning. The salon is highlighted with pink colors and decorated with stylized pictures of women. Her job is both productive labor (waged), yet also service work. Once again, Roseanne is feminized in her "pink collar" job.

Roseanne finds another job in the service industry as a server at the restaurant within Rodbell's, a department store. She wears a feminine uniform consisting of a dress with pink apron. She and her coworker, Bonnie, work under a manager with whom Roseanne has a contentious relationship. She remains at that job until the restaurant closes.

Finally, financial security befalls Roseanne as she opens a restaurant with a ten-thousand-dollar check given to her by her mother. Instead of using the money to pay bills, she—in consultation with Dan—decides to try to find long-term security instead of spending it in the short term. Co-owning the restaurant gives Roseanne the financial status she has been seeking throughout the run of the show. The diner serves "loose meat" sandwiches and caters to the working class of Lanford. Her ownership of the restaurant is a low-skill service job, but also involves management skills.

Most of the jobs Roseanne performs over the run of the show are low-level service jobs. She works on her feet all day and her wages are low (until she opens the diner). She struggles with finances as a working-class woman and depends on Dan to help make ends meet.

Roseanne's husband, Dan, worked in the construction field for many years, opened a motorcycle shop (that went under), managed a city garage, and then returned to the construction field. Both Roseanne and Dan struggled with unemployment, but Dan was more consistently employed and with higher wages.

Dan initially worked as a contractor for the first seasons of the show. His company, Four Aces Construction, kept him employed most of the year, but there were times when jobs were scarce. When a longtime friend gave him the part of the money to start his own motorcycle repair and sales shop, Dan jumped at the opportunity and took out a second mortgage on the Conner home to pay for his half. He worked at the shop restoring and selling classic Harley Davidson motorcycles, eventually employing Becky's boyfriend, Mark. Dan struggled to keep the shop open from the beginning. He had difficulty selling motorcycles and repair work was not as frequent as he had hoped. He was forced to close the motorcycle shop after he was unable to make payments on his loan, much to his devastation.

After a period of depression and unemployment, Dan finds a job managing the Lanford city garage. There he oversees the city fleet and the mechanics who fix it. This job was steady and had benefits (which were much needed at this point in the Conner family), but Dan found it boring and unrewarding. When he brought his son to the garage, DJ was disappointed in his dad's unexciting work. In "Construction Junction," Dan is faced with a dilemma: continue his manager job or go back into the construction industry with an exciting prospect. He chooses to return to construction.

The only workplaces of Dan ever portrayed on the show are the motorcycle shop and, rarely, the city garage. The motorcycle shop is constructed as a masculine place and the vast majority of the customers seen in the shop are male. When Roseanne and Jackie try to sell a bike out of desperation, they charm an uptight accountant into buying a motorcycle by telling him how manly he would be riding the Harley. Even David tries to become more masculine and bond with Dan when he contemplates getting a motorcycle. The city garage is also a masculine space. There are no female employees seen in the city garage. In fact, Dan's closest friends and son-in-law Mark seem to be the only workers (but that could be a contrivance of the show's writers). Mechanic work tends to be gendered male and the show represents that through both examples of the motorcycle shop and city garage.

In the sitcom *Murphy Brown*, Murphy Brown is a successful and famous television journalist who is known for her acid tongue, outrageous antics, and domineering behavior. She exudes masculinity right down to her name. The program centers on her job as an investigative journalist and anchor for the television newsmagazine *FYI*. The political satirical storylines were inspired by current events. *Murphy Brown* is set in the office and studio for the fictitious *FYI*. It is a brightly lit and somewhat clinical space. There is very little warmth or personality in the workplace.

Similar to the setting of the show, the character of Murphy is often seen as lacking warmth in her personality and demeanor. She is considered to be one of the boys and, in some cases, not a woman. She is successful in her career, despite it being a male-dominated industry. Coworker and senior anchor, Jim Dial, learns Murphy is pregnant in "Uh-Oh":

JIM: Murphy, do you need any money?
MURPHY: Jim, I make as much as you do.
JIM: Good God! Miles, is that true?

Murphy is frequently constructed as more masculine than her coworkers, even her male counterparts. She dominates her boss, Miles. Many times, in cases of conflict, Murphy will bypass Miles and go to his boss instead. Murphy's desire to get her own way and her desire for perfection in others led to the firing of ninety-three secretaries over the course of the show. In this aspect, Murphy is constructed as almost despotic and dictatorial in the workplace.

Murphy's masculinity constructs an image of Working Woman who cannot be feminine. Murphy's lone female coworker, Corky Sherwood Forrest, is stereotypically feminine (she is a former Miss America contestant) and is not as successful or well respected. The contrast between the two female characters constructs a successful Working Woman as one who sacrifices femininity for career advancement.[30]

The successful Working Woman is also constructed as without a personal life in *Murphy Brown*. Both Corky's and Murphy's marriages fail due to their high level of career involvement. Murphy's child, Avery, is taken care of by a nanny (albeit a male nanny). An interesting aspect of Murphy as a single working mom is that the conflicts between home and workplace are never an issue. Murphy's responsibilities to her child at home do not affect her responsibilities at work. Although her pregnancy affected her work schedule and her bout with breast cancer at the end of the show's run was a storyline, Murphy Brown is basically divorced from her personal/

domestic life while at work. Murphy's masculine traits reinforce the gender coding of the public workspace as a male domain. The complete separation of personal issues from the workplace only validates the dualism of associating the personal with private sphere.

The construction of Working Woman from *The Mary Tyler Moore Show* portrays nearly the opposite image as that found in *Murphy Brown*, but both constructions reinforce traditional notions of gender roles and patriarchally gendered codings of space. Both constructions designate the workplace as masculine and contribute to the masculinization of public space. *The Mary Tyler Moore Show* was considered revolutionary by many feminists when it appeared in 1970 due to its focus on a single working woman who was interested in a career, not just a job as a prelude to marriage.[31] Yet for all the feminist backing in 1970, the show constructed an image of a masculinized workplace and reinforced the association of masculine with the public sphere and productivity. This is done by the juxtaposition of the lead character, Mary Richards, with her boss, Lou Grant.

In the first episode of the show, Lou interviews Mary. She is told she was hired because she is a woman, not because she has the qualifications for the job. Mary's official job title is associate producer, but her duties are mostly secretarial. In fact, she makes less money as a producer than she would have as a secretary. Mary sacrifices money for her title, which only furthers serves to show that a Working Woman must make sacrifices, whether it is money or a personal life.

Mary's coworkers, including Lou, are constructed as a family. Mary performs either as daughter or mother when dealing with Lou and the rest of her coworkers. This only further associates the feminine with reproduction and negates Mary as Working Woman, constructing her in a reproductive (rather than productive) framework. Mary as the token female in the workplace is responsible for the fulfilling the typical female gender roles.

Visions of Gender

The constructions of Mother, Father, and Working Woman by the television sitcoms used in this analysis show the gender coding of space within the home and how they help to form gender identity. These constructions of gender ideals, although not monolithic, provide a guide for gender roles within the home and workplace and reinforce the gendered division of labor. These guides can be seen in episode after episode for nearly every sitcom chosen. Each socio-spatial construction of public and private spaces and their corresponding Mother, Father, and Working Woman roles should be related back to the context of the show. For the purposes of this analysis, examples are taken to show how these constructions lead to patriarchal codings of socio-spatial identities as well as gendered relations of (re) production.

It must be recognized that both television and gendered constructions of identity and gendered codings of space are not static and are always in flux. Television and its audience share a reciprocal relationship of influence and attention should be paid to the idea that television is intertextual. But it must be acknowledged that television is a powerful cultural tool that affects our daily lives, identities, and perceptions of space and place.

The medium of television has been disregarded in serious research due to its classification as low culture, which negates the power of television as a cultural force and its power to create cultural identities. Yet television helps to shape and create identity. Whether it is national, community, or gender identity, television influences how the audience perceives themselves, others and the space around them.

As shown through the examples from these various sitcoms, the medium of television constructs stereotypical categories of how men and women should act in space, whether the home or the workplace. This gendered coding of space only reinforces the patriarchal structure of feminizing private/reproductive spaces and masculinizing the public/productive spaces.

Although it promotes the dominant ideology of patriarchy, television also offers opportunities to resist, evade, and oppose it.[32] When these opportunities are taken, television works effectively as an instrument in destabilizing dualisms that reinforce gendered social relations of (re)production and promote patriarchal gender identities. These subversive efforts against the patriarchal norm certainly deserve commendation, but there needs to be more done to provide less stereotypical gender constructions and gendered codings of spaces.

Feminist geography needs to address the medium of television more directly due to the powerful forces of (re)production and the spaces in which these processes take place. Here I mean production as in the creation of television programming and reproduction as the multiplying of television's effects. The curation of images produced and reproduced on television affects the audience. These constructed and artificial images influence viewers and—through repetitive reinforcement—legitimize the patriarchal gendering of spaces and constructions of gender identity.

Embedded in the representations of (re)production is the idea of public privates. The public and private spaces portrayed within the chosen media texts show the eroding barriers between public and private. Whether an intimate and gendered portrayal of a home and the role of reproduction within its confines or the public space of workplace and the characteristics prioritized in production, the role of television in the formation of sociospatial identity is important to analyze.

Most American homes have at least one television, and with the variety of programming that television and mobile streaming devices offer, it provides something for virtually everyone ranging from the very young to the very old. It is a cultural influence that reaches predominantly into our private lives, the places where we feel most comfortable and secure. It is unlike other visual media due to its primary location in domestic spaces and our level of familiarity with it. Television's situation within the privacy of homes establishes an intimacy that requires examination and critique. We come to feel as if we know and identify with the characters we watch on television. This relationship is at the core of how television shapes social, cultural, and historical visions of gender.

5

Navigating Degrassi Community School

Socio-Spatial Identities in *Degrassi*

All iterations of Canadian teen drama *Degrassi* focus on life in the fictional world of Degrassi Community School in Toronto, Canada. The program started with *The Kids of Degrassi Street*, followed by *Degrassi Junior High*, *Degrassi High*, and *Degrassi: The Next Generation* (later called *Degrassi* and *Degrassi: The Next Class*). The focus of this chapter is on fourteen seasons of *Degrassi: The Next Generation/ Degrassi* (hereafter known simply as *Degrassi*). The series, created by Linda Schuyler (a former school teacher) and Yan Moore, plays on both U.S. and Canadian stations. It ran for fourteen seasons on television and started on Netflix for the fifteenth season onward. It is both critically acclaimed and popular, winning awards in both the United States and Canada. The series functions as a mix of educational and entertainment-focused television or what has been termed "edutainment."

The students at Degrassi Community School face many issues that teenagers face as they navigate high school in real life. Life at Degrassi

Community School reflects the lives of many teenagers today and the complicated situations in which they find themselves during junior and senior high school. It also presents an interesting televisual geography—a cultural glimpse into identity formation in the teen years. Using the private site of the body and the public setting of the school, this chapter focuses on how reel life reflects the real situations that many teenagers in the United States and Canada face. The actors are actual teenagers; many hired when they were around the age of thirteen. This set the series apart from its contemporaries (such as *Beverly Hills, 90210*; *90210*; *The OC*; and *Buffy the Vampire Slayer*), which cast people in their twenties to play teenagers. Former cast members have become international celebrities with careers in television and music (most notably, alumnus Aubrey Graham aka Drake).

The public space backdrop of the school is not unique to teenage-centered television programs, but the variety of topics is somewhat unusual for a show aimed at those in middle/junior high and high schools. While movies have focused on such issues, there has been a gap in television programming with the exceptions of perhaps *Beverly Hills, 90210* and its reboot, *90210*. While these programs feature older teens, *Degrassi* is based on grades seven through twelve. For example, the first two episodes deal with Emma and her Internet crush, Jordan. Twelve-year-old Emma arranges to meet up at a hotel with a teenage boy, who, in fact, turns out to be an adult Internet stalker/pedophile. Her mother and stepfather eventually rescue her. These first episodes set the tone for the series—that teenagers face serious issues and potential threats. Yet *Degrassi* doesn't function as a "very special episode" or a public service announcement.[1] Instead, it treats its characters as very real, very flawed humans that have to deal with difficult situations. Over the years, the series has dealt with such subjects as: rape, abortion, eating disorders, shootings, domestic violence, mental health topics, sex, self-mutilation, transgender issues, homosexuality, pregnancy, addiction, bullying, stalking, religious and racial discrimination, and death.

For the purposes of this chapter, I focus only on issues more directly related to body geographies: rape, pregnancy and abortion, coming out as homosexual and transgendered, and shootings, suicide, and death. Additionally, I examine only the first fourteen seasons of *Degrassi*. Because *Degrassi* has aired for so many years (and in so many different forms), it recycles plotlines and story arcs. However, these repeated stories do not become predictable because characters deal with similar situations differently.

Some scholars argue that all iterations of *Degrassi* portray a more genuine experience of the teenage years. Marie-Claire Simonetti argues that *Degrassi Junior High* is more "realistic" than *Beverly Hills, 90210*, stating that "both shows' narratives translate the values of the respective cultures: The American Dream conquers odds, whereas the Canadian ethos cautions against the very same odds."[2] Expanding on this idea, Suzanne Rintoul and Zachary Quintin Hewlett argue: "To be more precise, conversations about the series tend to reflect the idea that Canadian culture offers representations of youth and childhood that are somehow more authentic than, say, American television."[3] Comparisons such as these inevitably follow most examinations of *Degrassi*. While this chapter will not compare Canadian and American youth television programming, it is important to note that scholarship exists on the subject.

Degrassi explores adolescence as a complicated time. It is not simply school dances and crushes, but instead a time often fraught with anxiety, self-doubt, and peer pressure. *Degrassi* is confined by the genre, but also empowering for the audience. For Benjamin Lefebvre, "*Degrassi: The Next Generation* is particularly aligned with the constraints of adolescent problem fiction in terms of both its choice of subject matter and its discursive strategies: while most of the characters are complex and dynamic, individual scripts use them to enact social debates and to encode and personify abstract concepts about agency, identity, and power."[4] How *Degrassi* portrays identities socio-spatially will be the key theme examined here.

Intimate Acts in Public Spaces

Degrassi depicts a number of geographies during the run of the program. Both public and private spaces are key to the plotlines of the show. There is interplay between public spaces (such as the school) and private spaces (such as the body) in the series and in this analysis. As discussed earlier, the body can be both a public and private space with the interior of the body as the most intimate scale, but also serving as a public façade and representation. The school setting also serves as both a public and private space with the hallways and classrooms functioning as public spaces, while the bathrooms are more of a private public space.

The body is a complex site for geographical examination. Bodies are the quintessential public privates on which this book is focused. Within *Degrassi*, bodies are public-private spaces (both at once) on display at school and sometimes hidden within the home. How the body is represented in the public arena of school is an important aspect of this discussion. As children become young adults, their bodies are subject to a number of changes brought on by both puberty and peer pressure. Many of these changes are played out publicly in junior and senior high school, while also experienced at a very private level.

Bodies, especially those of children, are a topic that many people wish to avoid. Dealing with the sexual feelings and actions of children is even more taboo. For instance, when one of the characters (fourteen-year-old Manny) becomes pregnant, she chooses to terminate the pregnancy. Kate Aurther argues that abortion is still "television's most persistent taboo."[5] Yet Michele Byers argues that "abortion is *American* television's most persistent taboo."[6] The series does not shy away from these subjects. For Byers, "[*Degrassi*] story arcs about teenagers and sex are produced in a feminist framework that sees sexual knowledge as central to female empowerment, that recognizes self-determination about one's own body as an inherent right, and that places the question of 'choice' in the foreground."[7] The ways bodies are represented walk the line between treating teenagers as children or as young adults (e.g., see Susie Weller's work on young teenagers).[8] As teenagers, many face serious issues that have long-lasting effects.

Sexual Assault in the *Degrassi* Series

Twelve characters have been subject to some sort of sexual assault or threat in the series. Some characters were molested (Jane), others were sexually harassed (KC, Clare, Maya), and still others were raped (Paige, Darcy, Bianca, Zoe, Tristan) or assaulted in another way (Winston). In addition, Connor and Emma were nearly assaulted, but those attacks were prevented. While many of the assaults came from other students, there were cases in which teachers were the predators. For example, Mr. Yates was forced to leave Degrassi Community School after his relationship with Tristan was disclosed, as well as his groping of Winston. Other instances of adults taking advantage of students happen periodically as well. Paige becomes romantically involved with a student teacher at Degrassi and Coach Carson watches pornography with and hires a prostitute for an underage and uncomfortable KC. There are also cases of students acting improperly, such as when Darcy falsely accuses Mr. Simpson of an inappropriate student-teacher relationship. She later recants her story, but damages his career and reputation.

The character of Darcy is important to analyze as she exemplifies many of the topics I wish to explore in this chapter. Darcy Edwards takes pride in her Christianity, her virginity, and her spot on the Spirit Squad. She is romantically linked to a few boys at Degrassi Community School, but her major story arc deals with her relationship with Peter. In season seven, Darcy and Peter date without either having parental support. When Darcy and Peter go on a skiing trip with friends, he attempts to take their relationship beyond kissing. She asks him to leave her alone and then she goes to a party at the lodge with her friends to drown her sorrows. While she is in the bathroom, an unknown person spikes her drink. She becomes intoxicated and loses consciousness. A bit later in the episode, "Standing in the Dark," she is led into a bedroom by the still unknown person and raped. When she wakes up, she is naked next to Peter and believes they had sex. Peter denies this, but the rumor that they had sex runs rampant through Degrassi in the next few days. A humiliated Darcy is asked to give up her abstinence ring by her Christian-based group, the Friendship Club. Darcy soon learns that a "roofie rapist" worked the party at the lodge and she realizes—but does not admit to anyone—that the unknown person raped her. Suffering from depression and a case of chlamydia, she attempts suicide by slitting her wrists.

Darcy confides in Manny that she was raped and Manny keeps her secret, but tells Darcy that rape and sex are different. Darcy begins to become disruptive in class and is forced to see the school counselor. In an outburst, she reveals to a teacher, Mr. Simpson, that she was raped. Still acting out, she begins to flirt with Mr. Simpson and although the feelings are only on her side, she accuses him of sexually harassing her when she is rebuffed. Meanwhile, Peter ends their relationship and deems her "hopeless." When the truth about Mr. Simpson comes out, Darcy attempts jumping off the roof of the school, but is stopped by Manny. She is sent away to a camp for troubled teens and reunites with Peter. She finally admits that she was raped and that it was the root cause of her behavior. She eventually decides that to atone for her behavior she should go to Kenya to build schools during her senior year.

Darcy's body suffers multiple traumas during her time at Degrassi Community School. She is drugged and raped, leading to a sexually transmitted disease, depression, and two suicide attempts. Her experience is not unique in the real world and her reactions to her assault manifest in real ways although she is only a television character. Many teenagers can relate to her reel experiences in their real lives—some directly, others through the experiences of friends or family. The portrayal of these issues on television creates spaces of sympathy or empathy for many viewers.

The disruption of bodily boundaries (whether with drugs, sexual penetration, or other methods) is key to understanding why assault is so troubling at a personal level. The body, as the most intimate site we experience, is vulnerable and can be violated in a number of ways without consent. It is our most protected space, but subject to outside forces every day. The body is simultaneously a public and private space and, as such, provokes a constant negotiation between the two spheres. When the body's private interior is breached by exterior entities, it creates a metaphorical and/or literal leakage and this disruption can lead to depression and other feelings of anxiety surrounding the body.

When televisual bodies are disrupted on screen, they show the fragility of bodily boundaries. This can create unease in the viewer in multiple ways. Teenagers who view shows like *Degrassi* see how the televisual influences reality and how reality influences the televisual. In their lives, teenagers see the very real effects of disrupted bodily boundaries through their own personal experiences as well as those of their friends.

As mentioned earlier, other students at Degrassi Community School have been subject to predatory advances by others. The series does a service to viewers by showing that there are myriad ways in which one can be sexually assaulted and that none of them should be tolerated.

Another rape happens at Degrassi Community School in which other students are the offenders. Zoe Rivas attends Degrassi after a stint as a teenage television star. Zoe bullies other students and is not portrayed as a "nice" girl. Zoe attends a party one night after Drew breaks off their casual relationship. She drinks to excess and passes out. Luke and Neil then sexually assault her at the party. The assault is not seen on the show.

When Zoe wakes up the next morning at the party, she is naked under a blanket. Zoe is ignorant as to what happened and when she asked what she did the night prior, she gets slapped with "What didn't you do?" Zoe is then shown a cell phone filled with pictures of her partying and taking her clothes off. The photos had been circulated around the school and online. Zoe tries to figure out the events of the party as rumors flow.

When a video surfaces of two men raping Zoe, she realizes what has really happened to her. Although she does not remember any of it, she has video proof of her being assaulted while unconscious. Students at Degrassi begin to turn against her, accusing her of falsely describing a consensual situation as rape. As frustrations mount, she is confronted by one of her rapists who asks her to drop the case. Luke tells her that she "liked it" and states that no one will believe her if she continues to probe into what happened because he's "a good Christian guy" and sports star. He insists that this episode should not be allowed to ruin his life. Zoe eventually confronts Luke in the hallways of Degrassi and announces he was her rapist. Other students finally come to her defense as she attacks him with words and fists.

The case goes to trial and Zoe's name and history is exposed in the courts. In the episode "Believe," she responds to the character assassination in her victim's statement by saying: "I'm a mess, but you already know that. I've spent the last day listening to people say terrible things about me. I don't blame them. I made a lot of bad choices and probably going to make a lot more. I did not choose to be sexually assaulted. If you don't convict Luke Baker and Neil Martin today . . . then you're saying I deserved it. You're saying that other girls and boys, that they'll deserve it too. Well they don't. And I don't. I'm not sure I want to live in a world where that's true." She wins the court case.

Zoe is the first rape victim in the Degrassi franchise whose attacker was brought to justice. Paige's rapist was acquitted of charges due to lack of evidence, and Darcy's rapist was anonymous. Zoe is the third female character raped while at a party in addition to Paige (season two) and Darcy (season seven). She is also the third "mean girl" to be raped. Zoe is also the second rape victim to attempt suicide.

The portrayal of sexual assault and the aftermath for the victim shows sensitivity to what many teens face in reality. They may face backlash from their peers or the legal system. Their attacker may go free or have a light punishment. They may feel depression and want to end their lives. They may want to shake off the victim mantle and stand strong as survivors. All of these storylines have happened in *Degrassi* through depiction of violations of the body.

While rape is a violation of the most intimate, personal, and private nature, it can also be a public issue. In the case of *Degrassi*'s portrayal of sexual assault, the rapes become public knowledge within the school. It may be hidden at first (remaining private), but then as the plotline develops, it becomes more of a public story (e.g., the spreading of rumors, surfacing of videos, and suicides attempts all taking place at the school).

Pregnant Teenagers, Tough Choices

Other portrayals of the body occur in *Degrassi*. Pregnant bodies are seen as an aberration in most junior high and high schools. Degrassi Community School is no different. Yet teenage pregnancies happen in real life, much as they do at Degrassi. Each pregnancy storyline is treated differently and one in particular—that of Manny—was groundbreaking television.

Manny Santos was one of the original cast members of *Degrassi: The Next Generation*. Her character developed over the years from innocent child to a teenager with a promiscuous reputation. When Manny is initially rejected in her freshman year by a popular upperclassman, she decides to change her image from squeaky clean to "school slut." She starts wearing visible thongs, tight jeans, and skimpy tops, garnering attention from the boys at the school. Manny's closest friends, Emma and Liberty, confront her about her lack of self-esteem and essentially "slut shame" her for her behavior and attire. After the school principal forbids wearing thongs at school, Manny decides to go without underwear all together and cements her negative reputation at Degrassi.

After having a sexual relationship with Craig in "Holiday," Manny soon discovers she is pregnant at age fourteen. She confides in her best friend's mother (who also had a teenage pregnancy) who advises her to do what is best for her. When she tells Craig about the pregnancy, he is excited by the news and has fantasies of family life. However, Manny realizes that she is not ready to be a parent. Before the pregnancy is terminated, Manny's condition is revealed to the school. Manny tells her mother about the pregnancy, even though she fears that she will be sent to a convent like her cousin. Her mother is supportive, however, and drives her to the clinic for her abortion.

Manny's best friend, Emma, and the father, Craig, are devastated by the abortion. Emma is upset because she was the product of a teenage pregnancy and very likely could have been aborted. Emma comes around to support Manny as an act of friendship. Manny finishes her freshman year depressed and reclusive.

"Accidents Will Happen" framed abortion as a personal choice. This was quite revolutionary for a teen drama. *Degrassi* treats this episode as a teachable moment, but does so without preaching to the audience. It treats its characters and its viewers with respect by showing that life is full of complicated situations and decisions. The decision best for one may not be the best decision for another.

"Accidents Will Happen" was considered controversial in the United States. The N, the network on which *Degrassi* aired at the time, refused to broadcast the episode. The large amount of attention this censorship garnered from U.S. media led to the episode becoming a popular Internet download. So, in spite of not airing initially on network television, U.S. audiences saw the episode online and when season three was released on DVD.

Jenna Middleton also becomes pregnant during her tenure at Degrassi and chooses to keep the child. Jenna is a talented singer and songwriter, which led her to become a contestant on a fictional Canadian talent show during her pregnancy. Initially outgoing, she became depressed after placing her child with KC up for adoption.

Jenna finds out she is pregnant in "Tears Dry on Their Own" after gaining some weight and feeling sick. Her best friend urges her to take a pregnancy test, but Jenna initially refuses. Jenna is essentially in denial about her state, and her pregnancy is eventually five months along before she confirms it.

She breaks the news to the father, KC Guthrie. He tells her to get an abortion and they fight over the matter. When she realizes she is five months along and that abortion is not an option, she confronts KC again. He is enraged that she did not take a pregnancy test when she first thought she might be pregnant and yells at Jenna for her denial about the pregnancy. KC then breaks up with Jenna. After meeting up with and getting support from KC's mom, Jenna tells KC that he does not have to be involved unless he wants to be involved. He then hands her a book and they decide to get married (they do not go through with this) and raise the child as a family.

Jenna leaves Degrassi to take care of Tyson and soon resents KC for staying in school and hanging out with his friends. Jenna suffers from postpartum depression and struggles with raising the baby mostly on her own. Jenna moves in with the Guthrie family, which makes it easier for KC to help her. Jenna still struggles with being the primary caregiver.

Child Services comes to check up on Jenna, KC, and Tyson after a fight between Jenna and KC. Child Services is concerned about the environment in which Tyson is raised and tell Jenna that they may need take Tyson away. Jenna is home the next day changing Tyson's diaper as the Child Services representative observes Jenna and KC's parenting. Jenna asks about adoption and KC is shocked. They inform Child Services that they have some decisions to make.

In "Extraordinary Machine," Jenna and KC meet Tyson's possible adoptive parents. When Jenna leaves the room, KC tells his mother that he is reluctant to place his son for adoption. He decides to try to get Jenna to stay with him, but Jenna refuses. KC soon realizes the error of his ways and agrees to the adoption. They play with Tyson for one last time before giving him to his new parents.

Jenna and KC's situation, as compared to Manny's and others on the series, shows a teenage couple struggling with the decision to keep the child and parent as high schoolers. *Degrassi* depicts the difficulty of raising a child at such a young age, especially while trying to juggle school, work, and parenting. Jenna's pregnant body and resulting child create chaos in her life. Her social life, schooling, and career are all affected by her pregnancy. While to a lesser degree, KC shares many of her problems.

The plot lines of teenage pregnancy portrayed in Degrassi show a number of public privates. Geographies of body, home, and school are shown in these story arcs. The body is shown as not being one's own (hosting a fetus), but also paradoxically as within one's control (the right to terminate the pregnancy). The plotlines I have explored show very different outcomes for the female body.

They also show the home and family life of the characters involved. Parents are sometimes supportive, sometimes not. In Jenna's case, carrying the pregnancy to term and deciding to raise the child led to a burden that she (as the mother) bore instead of KC (the father). She was the one to give up school to raise the child while he attended classes. She was bound to the home, bound to the child, bound to reproductive duties. Many of the scenes in this arc take place in the home as it becomes a central focal point of Jenna and KC's story. In this case, childrearing becomes associated with the home and, overall, with Jenna as the mother. School, on the other hand, is a place of respite for father KC in the Jenna/KC story.

The arcs also show very different experiences for the young women at school. As just mentioned, Jenna left school after her child was born, while Manny remained enrolled and finished out her high school studies. While both Manny and Jenna received backlash from classmates when their pregnancies were revealed, ultimately Manny was able to reclaim Degrassi as a site of learning because of her choice to terminate the pregnancy.

Coming Out at Degrassi

Thirty-two characters, both major and minor, identified as homosexual, bisexual, or pansexual throughout the first fourteen seasons of *Degrassi*. This includes parents, teachers, coworkers, and fellow students. Many story arcs concerning these characters involve their "coming out" or disclosure of their sexual identity to others and how others react to these admissions. One student, Adam Torres, was outed as a transgender man.

Sexuality Disclosed

Marco Del Rossi was the first character on *Degrassi* to come out as gay. In season two, a major plotline is Marco's struggle to come to terms with his sexuality. He is confused about his feelings and attempts to date Ellie, his best friend, in order to fit in with his peers. Marco finally tells Ellie that he thinks he is gay after they kiss. Teased repeatedly by friend Spinner about his sexuality, Marco hides his true feelings by continuing to "date" a complicit Ellie as a cover. Soon after Ellie says she no longer can pretend to be Marco's girlfriend, Marco meets and is attracted to Dylan. His eventually coming out to close friends in season three is provoked by Spinner after Marco rebuffs a girl with whom Spinner has set him up. Spinner confronts him outside The Dot, the after-school hangout, and Marco confesses that he is gay. Spinner, repulsed and shocked, storms off, much to Marco's dismay and horror.

Spinner begins to bully Marco, calling him a "fag" and tagging his locker with homophobic and hate-filled graffiti. Jimmy, a black student, reprimands Spinner for his behavior and says that Spinner's homophobia is as bad as being racist. Marco is also gay-bashed for being in the "gay" part of Toronto. He lies about the assault initially, stating he was beaten because of his shoes, but then admits that it was because he was gay. Spinner ultimately realizes that his behavior was reprehensible and reestablishes his friendship with Marco, even helping Marco to ask out Dylan. Marco decides to run for class president in season four. His competitor, Alex, threatens to tell the whole school that he is gay. Alex decides not to reveal his secret, but Marco is still called "queer" when he gives his speech. All of Marco's close friends finally rally around him and support him during his coming out period. Although Marco is out to his close friends, he continues to hide his relationship with Dylan from his mother and father. Dylan breaks up with him, telling Marco that he needs to be open with his family.

Marco's father has a difficult time accepting homosexuality. In season four, Marco tells his mother he is gay and she is supportive. She embraces him with love, but acknowledges that his father will not react the same way, so she agrees to help him hide his sexuality from his father.

Meanwhile, Dylan and Marco reunite only to break up again while Dylan—away at college—asks for an open relationship. Marco tries to make Dylan jealous by kissing his heterosexual friend, Craig, but it does not work. It does, however, make Craig feel uncomfortable. Craig and Marco discuss the situation and work out the issue. Marco and Dylan break up shortly afterward because Marco decides he's uncomfortable with an open relationship.

Marco is attacked for sexual "immorality" by the Friendship Club (a Christian-based, abstinence club at Degrassi) in season five. He also finds a mentee in that season in Tim. Marco encourages Tim to come out to his father and he does, but Tim is dismayed to learn that Marco is closeted with his own father. To atone for this and to clear his own conscience, Marco comes out to everyone (his father included) at a school play. Marco's relationship with his father is strained because of his disclosure. Marco and Tim start dating, but it ends after Tim realizes Marco is using him to make his ex-boyfriend jealous. Marco and Dylan reunite soon after Tim and Marco break up.

Marco has several romantic relationships as the series progresses, some more important than others. The degree to which Marco's romantic life is fleshed out is important to note. Marco is portrayed much as the other characters are. Heterosexual characters fall in and out of love and so does Marco. The fact that Marco's love life is normalized is an important moment in television.

The story of Marco portrays geographies of the body and geographies of sexuality. While he is at first harassed by some of his fellow students, most accept him as a colleague or friend. His body becomes a site of violence when he is "gay bashed" in the streets of Toronto. His sexuality, of course, factors into this. The series helps to depict homosexuality and the dating life of a homosexual teen as normal. As such, many teenagers can identify with Marco (and other characters that identify as homosexual, bisexual, or pansexual) and see some of their experiences on screen. It can also show that one's peers and family can accept one's sexuality, while also showing the stigma and shunning that may occur from those same groups.

Gender Revealed

Adam Torres (born Gracie) is a female-to-male (FTM) transgender teen. He transfers to Degrassi to escape transphobic bullying at his former school. Adam initially tries to blend in and not stand out, but after exposure as a transgender man, that was impossible. Eventually, he discovers that he could be himself and still maintain meaningful and close friendships.

"I Just Don't Know What to Do With Myself" introduces students at Degrassi (and viewers of *Degrassi*) to Adam. He is portrayed as a normal, somewhat rambunctious teen until viewers are let in on his secret in "My Body Is a Cage." In that episode, Adam flirts with Bianca until the beginning of his menses interrupts him. He abruptly leaves Bianca to retrieve tampons from his locker. He hides them from public view as he makes his way to the restroom until he bumps into a female student, Clare, and drops them. When two male students pass by, Adam feigns disgust and pawns the hygiene products off as Clare's. Clare follows the ruse.

Later in the episode, Adam looks at his reflection in the mirror. As he turns to one side, viewers see that he has breasts and is FTM. He binds his breasts and puts on his shirt to cover the bandages. Drew, his brother, enters the room after joking how Adam took less time to get ready when he was a girl. Drew then asks if Adam thinks Clare said anything to anyone about the tampon situation (she did mention them to her friend, Eli). Their mother shouts from downstairs that the two need to get ready and calls Adam "she." Adam responds: "Pronoun problems? Still, mom?" She apologizes and calls them down again.

The next day, Adam overhears Clare and Eli discussing how he had tampons. Adam goes over to the table at which they are sitting and explains how he was born in a girl's body, and how he is FTM. Eli responds positively and jokes about whether or not this means he can "rip one" in front of him. The three then laugh and have lunch together

Adam again tries to flirt with Bianca. It initially goes smoothly until Bianca touches his chest. Bianca rips open his shirt to reveal the binding around his chest, thus outing him. Adam bolts to the men's restroom and two classmates follow him and harass him. They then throw Adam against a door. Drew comes in and attempts to break up the fight, eventually getting entangled with one of the assailants. Drew is punched, while the other student prevents Adam from helping out his brother. Later, the Torres family meets with the principal to discuss the fight and to demand that the bullying stop or they will transfer to another school. She points out how transgender students often receive death threats or are assaulted. The principal states that the offenders have been suspended, but then decrees that Adam needs an escort to classes and must use the handicapped bathroom.

Adam sits next to Clare and Eli in his classes and tells them that his family has a hard time accepting him as a male. He mentions that he will have to be "Gracie" when his grandmother visits. When Adam goes shopping with his mother in anticipation of his grandmother's dinner visit, he picks up a plaid men's shirt and asks if he can wear it. She shakes her head and picks out a white girls' shirt instead. Adam mentions that he has thought about "introducing Adam to Grams." Mrs. Torres responds that maybe he should forgo dinner. At the dinner, Gracie appears and plays the role of granddaughter.

Adam decides that life was easier as Gracie. He then shows up to school as Gracie although it torments him to live his life that way. Adam begins to burn himself again in an act of self-mutilation. Clare catches him in the act and begins to comfort him. She goes on to say that he does not have to be Gracie if it doesn't make him happy. Adam responds that it makes everyone else happier, so he needs to make the change. Clare says that he is not the one who needs to change.

Adam returns to his male clothing. He asks his mother what she sees when she looks at him: boy or girl. Mrs. Torres says girl and Adam asks her to see him as her son. Adam decides to light a bonfire to move forward with his life as a male and burn Gracie's clothes. When Mrs. Torres gives

Adam a photograph of Gracie holding a book, Adam refuses to burn it because he feels that it's a part of him who he is.

Adam and frenemy Fitz are lifting weights in "Purple Pills" when Adam is unable to lift some of the weights. Adam becomes angered and states that he wants to fight. Fitz invites Bianca over to fight with Adam, stating, "No guy is going to want to punch a girl." Adam runs off, saying he is "not a girl." He later punches Fitz in the stomach, throws him down, and promises he will fight him later. Clare and Eli try to convince Adam not to fight, but he persists. Clare eventually stops the fight by setting off the smoke alarm at the school.

Adam joins the school play (*Romeo and Juliet*) and becomes attracted to fellow student Fiona. While they rehearse one day at Fiona's house, a nervous Adam tells her he is transgender. Adam expects backlash, but Fiona simply nods her head and says "okay." Surprising him, Fiona says she does not care and prefers kissing him to any other guy at Degrassi. They become a couple, break up soon after, and then reconcile.

After they get back together, Fiona makes a pass at Adam that makes him feel uncomfortable with his body. To smooth things over, Fiona says that she likes that Adam is "the best of both worlds" because he's "boyish and girlish." This angers Adam because he does not wish to be reminded of his female parts. He then learns Fiona is a lesbian and is just using him. Adam then leaves, telling Fiona that she should accept that she wants to be with women.

In "Cry Me a River," Adam mimics another student in the men's restroom. Adam stares and tries to copy his stance, which frightens Dave. Adam apologies and explains that he recently purchased a stand-to-pee device. Dave returns to the restroom later in the afternoon only to be followed by Adam again. At the urinal, Dave is curious as to how Adam can use the urinals. He looks at Adam and asks about the device. Surprised, Adam drops the device on the floor and splashes Dave. Dave leaves the restroom, instructing Adam to stay away. Dave calls Adam a "tranny" on the student radio station in retaliation. Other students admonish him for his transphobic actions. Adam explains to Dave that he cannot change his identity as FTM. Dave apologizes.

Adam attempts dating girls at Degrassi, but is rejected or ends relationships quickly, although most seem fine with his gender identity at first. After one rejection, Adam seeks counseling about a mastectomy. He needs to go through counseling in order to be eligible for the surgery, but the counselor says that his body is still changing and gives Adam a better binder for his breasts instead.

One relationship lasts longer than an episode or two—Becky. Becky likes Adam and does not care that he is transgender. Becky asks Adam to be her "secret boyfriend" because she is afraid her parents will drive them apart, but not because he is transgender. They seal their newly minted relationship with a kiss. Adam eventually meets Becky's parents (she cannot keep a secret) and after they discover he is FTM, they try to convert him back to being a girl. Becky minds her parents' wishes and ends her relationship with Adam. She later tries to reconcile. After initially rebuffing Becky, he changes his mind and they begin to date again. They have a tumultuous relationship and Adam loses trust in Becky. They break up again during a fight over Adam's invasion of her privacy. While camping, Adam receives a text message from Becky reading, "Adam. I'm sorry. We should talk." He drives out of the woods for better cell service as he texts back to her "I <3 u Becky." He then crashes, distracted by his texting. Adam dies as a result of the accident.

Adam was the first transgender character ever to be featured on *Degrassi* as well as the first transgender person to be a main character in Canadian television history. Additionally, Adam was the first scripted teenage FTM character in television history (not including one-time guest roles).

When Adam died, GLAAD's Wilson Cruz issued the following statement: "When *Degrassi* introduced its large and loyal audience to Adam Torres, an authentic, multi-dimensional transgender character, the show not only made television history, but set a new standard industry standard for LGBT inclusion. With so few transgender characters on television, we are disappointed that Adam's story had to end this way, and we hope other shows will follow *Degrassi*'s lead in bringing stories like his to viewers."[9] After the backlash, Linda Schuyler (one of the show's creators) defended the choice to kill the character, stating: "The combination of Adam being a favorite character, and Jordan being at the end of her contract, presented a unique opportunity to tell this story through such a beloved character. As saddened as we are to say goodbye to Adam, we feel this storyline will affect even more lives in an authentic way."[10]

The key geographies in Adam's story revolve around the body and public-private site of the school restroom. Adam's body was a contested site in regard to gender—some wanted him to be a girl, he was a boy. This struggle played out in the series and showed the very real conflict that can happen for transgender teens. His body and his gender confused some of his peers, while others accepted his gender without a second thought.

Restrooms have become a "battleground" in the fight for transgender equality both in reality and on screen. For Adam, the restroom was a place of conflict, of assault—analogous to the experiences of many transgender teens today. He had very little respite from classmates there and was bullied in that site. His attempts to live a "normal" life were often thwarted by his peers in the Degrassi Community School restroom. As a result, the restroom became a place of oppression and fear. This is not dissimilar to current political movements in the United States. There has been a recent movement to discriminate against transgender persons through institution of a law that would force them to use the restroom of their "sex" instead of their "gender."

The portrayal of a transgender character—and a teen to boot—is a revolutionary moment in television history. Many teens may identify with Adam, and his story may resonate with their own, leading to a manifestation of the reel/real.

Death and Violence at Degrassi

Shootings at Degrassi Community School happen with some shocking regularity, much as they do in today's society. Five characters have been shot on the series: Jimmy Brooks, Sean Cameron, Gavin "Spinner" Mason, Adam Torres, and Rick Murray (fatally). Rick shot Jimmy in season four after peer bullying pushed Rick beyond his limits. Both Rick and Sean were shot as they struggled to gain possession over Rick's gun. Spinner was struck in the shoulder during a robbery at The Dot, as was Adam at a school dance ("Dead and Gone").

The shooting that involved Rick, Jimmy, and Sean was especially shocking to the *Degrassi* world. The situation leading up to it was complicated and the series explored it through a complex story arc. In season three, Rick dated Terri MacGregor and their relationship became abusive when Rick's jealousy could not be controlled. He accused Terri of favoring Jimmy over him and hurt her repeatedly. Although she broke off the relationship at one point, Terri took him back after he established trust with her again a few months later. Terri tries to convince her doubtful friends that he has changed. She defends Rick to her friends, but he misinterprets the situation and pushes her to the ground where she hits her head on a cinder block resulting in a coma. Terri transferred to a private school after recovery.

Rick returns to Degrassi after being expelled and reinstated in season four. He is bullied because of his treatment of Terri. Rick soon is subject to violence similar to that he inflicted upon Terri. Emma initially leads the school in protest against Rick's return, but changes her mind when she sees him beaten by other students. Jimmy eventually begins to let up on his bullying of Rick when they become teammates in an academic competition.

During the competition finals, Rick becomes the target of a cruel prank set up by students Jay, Spinner, and Alex. As he wins the competition for Degrassi, yellow paint and feathers pour over him. Humiliated, he leaves the competition and heads home. At home, he retrieves his father's handgun and returns to Degrassi to shoot those who have tormented him. After a student expresses her disgust at the prank, he heads to the lavatory and begins to clean up, seemingly deciding to abort the shooting spree. When Jay and Spinner enter, Rick hides in a stall and overhears them lying about who was responsible for the prank (they blame Jimmy).

Now on the hunt for Jimmy and Emma (who had rejected his affections earlier), he walks through the hallways with gun in hand. Rick confronts Jimmy and shoots him in the back as Jimmy realizes what is happening and runs away. Rick then tries to find Emma, encountering Sean, Toby, and her. As Toby spies the gun and urges the trio to flee, Rick points the gun and yells: "Don't turn away from me!" Sean attempts to calm Rick down, but is unsuccessful. Sean tries to wrestle the gun away from Rick after he points it at Emma and both are shot in the struggle. Rick dies from the gunshot and Sean is injured. Sean struggles with what happens and leaves Degrassi Community School. Jimmy is paralyzed from the waist down. Spinner is wracked with guilt and confesses to Jimmy that he is indirectly responsible for his paralysis:

SPINNER: When that paint was dumped on Rick, we told him that you did it.

JIMMY: And then he shot me . . .

Jimmy then rolls away in his wheelchair and leaves Spinner alone in the gym.

The second death of a regular character occurs in season six with the murder of Degrassi senior JT Yorke. In "Rock This Town," a house party goes horribly awry when JT argues with a student from a rival high school that had recently merged with Degrassi. JT encounters Drake Lempkey and another student urinating on his car. When JT makes light of the situation with the statement "You slay me with your humor" and begins to walk away, Drake comes up behind him and stabs him with a pocket knife. As he stabs JT, he says "Oh yeah, mascot boy? Laugh at this!" JT's former girlfriend, Liberty, finds him and she calls for help. At the hospital, JT is pronounced dead. Students mourn at Degrassi in different ways. The school erects the JT Yorke Memorial in the Degrassi Zen Garden and his closest friends leave a cap there at what would have been his graduation.

The third death of a major character happens six seasons later. When Campbell "Cam" Saunders commits suicide in season twelve's episode "Bittersweet Symphony," some viewers criticized the reaction by the characters for not being emotional enough. Cam was not given a eulogy that one might expect. The eulogy was filled with anger. The decision by the writers and producers to show the devastation left behind by Cam was deliberate. Their focus was to show how suicide affects those left behind and not to glorify or glamorize it.

Cam's death did not come without warning. Cam suffered from depression and stress related to school, relationships, and sports. His depression, loneliness, and anxiety were foreshadowed throughout the first half of season twelve. He jumped off a railing while at school, breaking his arm. He lost interest in the sport he once loved (hockey) and his personality was volatile with extreme mood swings.

Suicide is a recurring theme in the *Degrassi* series: Cam committed suicide and seven students have attempted suicide over the fourteen seasons analyzed here: Craig Manning (season two) Sean Cameron (season four), JT Yorke (season five), Darcy Edwards (season seven), Ellie Nash (season eight), Mike Dallas (season twelve), and Zoe Rivas (season thirteen).

As discussed earlier, Adam dies unexpectedly after a car accident brought on by texting. He crashed into a tree while returning a text. He succumbs to his injuries in the hospital. His friends and family reel from grief and the school holds a moment of silence for him at his expected graduation ceremony. Adam is the seventh character to die in *Degrassi* (besides Craig Manning's father Albert [a minor character], Rick, JT, Anson [a minor character], Cam, and Paula [a minor character]) and the second character to die from a car accident (Albert Manning was the first).

The deaths of students at Degrassi Community School show the fragility of life, even at such young ages. Their deaths mean the ultimate demise of their bodies. Dying is an intimate act and these deaths have been played out publicly on the television screen. The termination of life, especially lives of teenagers and children, can cause viewers to contemplate their own mortality.

The violent means by which many of them have died reflects violence in society. Creator Linda Schuyler has stated that she was profoundly affected by the Columbine shootings and other school shootings and felt a need to express the horror of the violence inflicted upon those students. The terror of shootings affected both the actors and the audience profoundly.

The issues surrounding death at Degrassi are complicated—as they should be. They involve situations such as dealing with the aftermath of sexual assault, bullying, abuse, and depression. These are issues that teenagers face in their everyday lives. Their portrayal shows that those who struggle with bullying or mental health issues are not alone.

Graduating from Degrassi

The *Degrassi* series tries to capture the teenage experiences of urban Canadian youth. At the same time, it is relevant to a larger, global audience. *Degrassi* shows a variety of teenagers in their struggles through high school. They deal with love, friendship, bullying, and discrimination in their daily lives. These issues are often reel representations of those that real students face. These representations portray a number of social and cultural geographies that influence viewers. *Degrassi*, in one iteration or another, has broadcast since 1979. The series has resonated with viewers since its inception. The actors are like the people you saw in the halls at school, with whom they share lockers and gossip, and who are friends and enemies. Actors are also the actual age of the characters they play. There have been new cohorts of students each year as viewers said goodbye to graduating seniors. *Degrassi* tried to be "real."

But aside from being the anti–*90210*, *Degrassi* was also the first high school show to not trivialize the teenage years. The kids of Degrassi Community School faced real issues, just like you did. From school shootings and teenage pregnancies to drug abuse and eating disorders, no topic is or was off limits on *Degrassi*.[11] Schwartzberg argues that "as such shows about teens go, it's always been a uniquely intelligent and honest series about young people. It is perhaps the most impressive example of this particular genre."[12] The series seems more genuine than other shows of the genre because it touches on storylines from which other programs shy away. It is open-minded about its characters and their choices.

The geographies of the show reflect the geographies of teens today. They navigate school and their peers on a daily basis. They are supported and challenged in their endeavors to become adults. They face issues that affect their bodies and their minds daily. The hallways they walk at school become spaces of love and hate, of friends and foes. They are subject to peer pressure based on how they look, act, or love. Degrassi is a show with which viewers identify because the stories they see on screen show them that they are not alone.

6

Big Brother Is Watching You

Why You Should Be Watching Reality TV

We are awash in a sea of reality television. All over the globe, reality TV reigns. "Reel" shows that depict "real" life are important to examine due to the impacts of representation. This chapter analyzes representations of three categories of bodies in reality television: confined bodies, "model" bodies, and bodies in motion. I use examples from shows such as *Big Brother (BB)*, *America's Next Top Model (ANTM)*, and *So You Think You Can Dance (SYTYCD)*.

These programs are popular with audiences worldwide as international versions of each of these shows exist and continue to have strong ratings. The U.S. version of *Big Brother* pulls in five to seven million viewers each episode. *America's Next Top Model* airs in 186 countries and there are versions of the show in over twenty-five countries (e.g., *Singapore's Next Top Model* and others). The programs chosen for this work are shown at least once a week for the duration of their cycles on both network and cable stations. Ratings typically fluctuate somewhat from year to year, but these programs have had consistently strong audience showings for over a decade.

There is usually a format to many of the competition-based shows (such as the programs explored in this chapter). Typically one or two contestants are eliminated each week after an audience or panel vote. Many incorporate "confessionals" or additional footage in which contestants are able to voice concerns or thoughts in a private space. This often provides context for the "plot" of each episode.

For the purpose of this chapter, I use a binary of scripted and reality television. This dichotomy is a false one as many reality shows are "scripted" to some degree or have strong producer influence, but the dualism is necessary in order to distinguish between the two styles of television. Many reality television shows are moving toward calling themselves "unscripted" because of heavy backlash to the label of "reality"—with many critics arguing that being followed by a camera and filmed is not a reflection of "real" life.

Many people state that the contestants on some of these reality shows are "fame-hungry" or "would do anything to be on camera." While this may be true in some cases, it is not the focus of my argument here. It is important to note that many reality show participants do continue on to other reality programs and experience some form of celebrity (whether positive or negative attention) as a result of their television experience.

While *ANTM* has not yielded a household name supermodel (like Tyra Banks herself), contestants from *ANTM* and *Big Brother* have parlayed their initial reality show appearances into additional shows and opportunities, like *Survivor* or *The Amazing Race*. Dancers that competed in past seasons of *SYTYCD* have returned to the show to work as all-stars or as judges, have appeared in movies (such as the *Step Up* series), and have been hired to work as professional dancers and choreographers on Broadway or on other reality dance competitions, such as *Dancing with the Stars*.

While fame and celebrity seeking is an important criticism of reality television participants, this chapter is more concerned with representations of bodies in this type of programming. My argument here is that the bodily geographies represented by unscripted television programming both reinforce and destabilize (often at the same time) social constructions of what bodies look like and do. In other words, television, especially unscripted television, produces an understanding of the real world through its produced images of bodies in the reel world.

Bodily Geographies

The body is both private and public at the same time. The boundary of the body contains the private, but exhibits a public façade. This chapter, as does this book, examines the public-private aspects of the body but focuses more on the public presentation of bodies on television. The three television programs that I use primarily for this chapter are *America's Next Top Model*, *Big Brother*, and *So You Think You Can Dance*. Each show is used as a case study for a different category of body: the confined body, the "model" body, or the body in motion. These bodies highlight multiple spatial elements and show how social norms are acted out on the body and through representations of the body.

Confined Bodies

Starting with MTV's *The Real World*, strangers have been asked to live together and let their every action be filmed. In fact, the opening to each episode of *The Real World* states: "This is the true story of seven strangers picked to live in a house, work together and have their lives taped, to find out what happen when people stop being polite and start getting real . . . *The Real World*." *The Real World* is often credited for launching the modern reality television genre.

One of *The Real World*'s offspring, *Big Brother*, follows a similar format. *Big Brother* contestants remain sequestered in a house outfitted with cameras for around ninety days in the hopes of winning a $500,000 prize. They are monitored twenty-four hours a day. Everything competitors say is recorded and everything they do is broadcast live via Internet and television feeds. They have no news from the world outside of the house. The only exception to this component of the game was after the events of September 11, 2001.

Most houseguests on *Big Brother* are attractive (some are models or pageant winners), thin or athletic, young, and white. They are predominantly heterosexual and cisgendered (their sense of personal identity and gender matches their birth sex). There are a few outliers to this. Racial and ethnic diversity are most common, followed by sexuality. Most houseguests are in their twenties, but a few have been teenagers and a very few have been older than their thirties. *Big Brother* houseguests do not reflect the diversity of the American viewing audience, but they do reflect an image of beauty that is standard on unscripted television.

There are numerous competitions held throughout the sequestering period. They are Head of Household (HOH), Power of Veto (POV) and the Have/Have Not competitions. These are either physically or mentally taxing events. Some have both physical and mental components (like jumping on a trampoline in order to memorize a scene and then running back to re-create the memorized scene). Others are endurance challenges. During the first HOH competition of *Big Brother 15*, the contestants hung on gigantic popsicles and were licked by a giant tongue for hours and doused by colored water while they spun about the house's backyard.

Contestants have a weekly Have/Have Not competition in which they try to avoid becoming a Have Not. Have Nots have food restrictions; for example, one week Have Nots could only eat habañeros, sardines, and "slop" (oatmeal with protein added), take cold showers, and sleep in uncomfortable conditions (airline seats, bumper cars, and so on). The physical discomforts the Have Nots are meant to endure physically weaken the body and often lead to emotional outbursts from the restricted houseguests. They are provided with basic needs, but it is meant to be a very severe physical punishment for the losing houseguests. Some houseguests will spend multiple weeks at a time as a Have Not. One hypoglycemic houseguest fainted after only being allowed to eat slop.

It is not just bodies that are sequestered in *Big Brother*; the nonphysical social and psychological makeup of each participant is affected as well. The confined bodies of *Big Brother* compete to outlast each other in the house. The physical stress does take its toll on their bodies somewhat, but they typically remain healthy (if not hungry on slop weeks). The toll that the confinement of their bodies takes on their mental faculties is quite astounding. The mental endurance required to live in isolation from the outside world with a group that is actively trying to evict you from the house so that they may win the prize is considerable. Sometimes people snap. In at least five seasons of the U.S. edition of *Big Brother*, houseguests have been expelled for violence or warned for violent actions. They range from placing a knife against another guest's throat to destruction of house property. One houseguest used another's toothbrush to clean the toilet and returned it without its owner's knowledge. *Big Brother* producers stepped in to prevent the toothbrush from being used further.

There have been numerous occasions where outlets have been needed to deal with the tension of the house. Houseguests have had sex in multiple seasons of *Big Brother* in both the U.S. and international versions. In fact, sex on a season of *Big Brother Africa* led to criminal charges for one houseguest based on Ethiopian law. While there has been no homosexual sex on the U.S. version of the show (unlike for other countries), there have been a number of heterosexual couples (called "showmances") that have engaged in the act. Some are overt, some try to be discrete. Masturbation also transpires on camera. Again, some acts are overt, some discrete. While the main television audience is not privy to these "private" acts carried out publicly on camera, those subscribers that watch the live feeds on the Internet see these acts as they occur and often will post them to various entertainment news sites.

While their sexual acts are aired on the Internet feeds without censoring, the confined bodies of *Big Brother* are allotted a modicum of privacy when they are showering or eliminating waste. A frosted glass window in the shower provides some privacy while still allowing some access to the cameras. While there is a camera in the stall of the bathroom, there is a solid door that gives some relief from the other cameras and the other houseguests.

There have also been instances of discrimination in the house based on race, gender, and sexuality. Misogynistic, racist, and homophobic remarks have been uttered and, of course, captured on camera, in multiple seasons of *Big Brother*. During *Big Brother 15*, contestants were fired from their jobs outside the house due to their comments and actions inside the house. They did not know that they had lost their jobs until after they were evicted, in order to protect the premise of the show. This is one case of the public depiction of private feelings and actions affecting livelihoods. The public-private world of *Big Brother* has affected the nongame world. When one houseguest's egregious comments were read back to her during her eviction interview, she claimed that (1) she didn't say them, and then (2) that they were taken out of context. The host quickly reminded her that she was recorded twenty-four hours a day and that everything she said was available "in context" and streamed via live internet feeds.

Big Brother is a game in which the whole body is used. It is physically and mentally taxing on the houseguests. They are filmed constantly with no reprieve—they know that, of course, when they sign up—but somehow they forget about the omnipresent cameras and microphones. The house forms a microcosm in which people interact constantly with one another because (1) they are forced to do so, and (2) because there is nothing else to do.

The confinement of bodies in the case of *Big Brother* can elucidate much about society. Not only do the houseguests form a delicate social fabric, they reflect social and cultural values. The confinement is key to this. They are isolated from society and tested to mental and physical breaking points. Because of this, they provide a unique case study to discuss body norms in a space that lacks virtually all privacy. They have no reprieve from one another, and hence, they have no reprieve from the social. They must constantly interact in a public manner without the luxury of private space.

The "Model" Body

America's Next Top Model is a show created and hosted by Tyra Banks up until 2017 when Rita Ora took over hosting duties (Banks will resume in later cycles). Banks is an African American supermodel who has been featured in numerous magazines from *Sports Illustrated* to *Vogue* throughout her career. She, a panel of judges, and a creative director mentor the young models as the premise of the show. The models are overwhelmingly in their early twenties or late teenage years (later cycles will eliminate the age limit). The first nineteen cycles featured women or transgendered women only, while the twentieth and twenty-first cycles featured men and women. The models live together in an apartment or house (called the Top

Model House) in Los Angeles or New York City during the duration of competition until five to six models are left. They then go to an alternate location, usually abroad. These locales have been destinations in Hawaii (U.S.), Europe, Africa, Australia, South America, and Asia.

The models that compete on the show go through a casting and audition process in which their looks and personalities are evaluated. There is a short interview followed by the potential competitor walking a "runway walk" in a swimsuit or underwear and posing for a panel of judges. The judges then evaluate the model's potential and sort her into a ranking system. Their runway walk, audition photographs, personality, and posing are all considered.

Once they enter the competition, a weekly challenge that teaches the models an essential skill in modeling and a photo shoot are used as criteria to judge the contestants each week. The final segment of the show is the judging and elimination of a contestant. The "top photo" of the week is called out first and then the models are called in descending order to walk a runway in order to be handed their photos from Banks. The two bottom contestants are called up together and after Banks delivers a speech describing their strengths and weaknesses, at least one model is eliminated and sent home (or to the limbo world that reality contestants go to before they actually go home so as not to spoil the results of the show).

Banks often will state that the women of the show are not always traditionally beautiful. They may have large ears or foreheads ("five-heads" is a Banks-ism) or gaps in their teeth. Banks argues that their beauty comes from their faces or bodies being interesting. She often will criticize models for being too commercially attractive, too conventionally beautiful. In casting, Banks is often seen as looking for quirks or unusual traits that will cause a model to stand out. Furthermore, Banks likes to discuss a style she calls "ugly-pretty." It is a look in which an ugly face is reined in just a bit so as not to be seen as grotesque, but visually interesting and stimulating to the viewer.

That being said, the women featured in the first twenty-two cycles of *ANTM* are mostly standard models (smaller than U.S. size two), while a handful of plus-size models (over U.S. size six were included in the competition. The winner of cycle ten, Whitney, was the only plus-size finalist. Banks, in later cycles, describes plus-size models as "fiercely real." Often judges eliminate "fiercely real" contestants because they've "lost their spark" or some other personality evaluation. In one standout elimination, the cycle three panel of judges sent a "fiercely real" contestant home because they deemed her vibrant personality as diminishing. They argued that plus-size models need their personalities more than standard models.

One cycle was deemed the "petite" cycle in which contestants were five feet, seven inches or under. Petite models have to find a niche market similar to plus-size models. Only certain agencies will contract petite models. There was a strong emphasis on personality during that cycle as well. Banks and her fellow judges argue that personality is more important for models that deviate from the standard.

America's Next Top Model covers eating disorders as an issue periodically. There have been a few notable instances where models struggled with eating disorders during the run of the show. Those women were eliminated from the competition relatively early on. Judges, in their evaluations of these women, state that they are too unhealthy (both mentally and physically) to continue competing or are sending the wrong message about the modeling industry. Judges typically question the models on whether they mentally can handle the difficulties of modeling. There is always concern over whether the women are mentally stable enough to withstand the constant criticism and competition of the fashion industry.

America's Next Top Model highlights a number of sociocultural identities through the contestants that the producers and judges choose to compete. These include race, gender, and sexuality. Women of color on the show are often asked about the lack of representation of their race or ethnicity on magazine covers. They too are asked if they can mentally handle the stress of representing their race/ethnicity in the competition or in the modeling world.

There have been two transgender contestants on *ANTM*: Isis in cycles eleven and seventeen (all-stars) and Virgge (cycle twenty). Isis had not undergone surgery in cycle eleven, but the surgery was performed in 2009 and her transition to female was complete when she competed in cycle seventeen. Virgge left the competition before final casting, citing health issues due to the hormones she was taking. Producers highlighted the struggles of the transgendered models who competed. "Tucking and taping" was often an issue for Isis in swimsuit shoots.

Lesbian and bisexual models feature on the show as well. Some of the women are out before the show, some realize their sexuality during the course of the show, while others disclose it at some point without fanfare. Often some of the other models fear that the lesbian or bisexual woman in the house will try to make sexual advances on them or find sexual gratification from being nude around the women. This fear is often a "story arc" at first, then quickly fades.

The physical discomfort producers ask the contestants to endure for photo shoots is a repeated theme throughout the run of the show. Many models express that "modeling is a lot harder than it looks," or some variant of that statement. They wear restrictive clothing or sometimes nothing at all. They wear extreme fashion (like fetish clothing for one shoot or six-inch platform heels for a challenge). They interact with insects (like cockroaches and silkworms), and spiders and snakes are used as accessories.

A dance element is often incorporated into the show as well. From hip-hop hula to traditional Thai dancing, the models are taught to move their bodies. This is to improve their "dance" with the camera and the photographer. The models learn to be aware of the angles of their face and how light plays off of their faces and bodies. The judges state repeatedly that control and movement of bodies as well as a hyperawareness of how one looks on film is critical to modeling. Interestingly, models are often asked to be more than a pretty face and to show emotion or understanding in their eyes.

One key show in each cycle is the makeover show. Models are given haircuts or extensions and weaves. Sometimes Banks orders that heads be shaved. Hair color is altered slightly with highlights or dramatically from black to icy blond. Straight hair becomes curly and vice versa. Eyebrows are shaped and bleached and sometimes the women are outfitted with contacts or their teeth are repaired with dental veneers. In one case, a dentist widened a women's gap between her teeth to make her look unique. Models often respond dramatically to these changes. Many cry when stylists make the first cut or the razor comes out. Some embrace their new look; others feel uncomfortable with Banks's vision of them and seek to put their own stamp on their looks by modifying their hairstyles on their own.

America's Next Top Model, as a show about modeling, is focused on appearances of bodies. While superficial to some, the bodies portrayed can tell us about social understandings of the body. Bodies on the program are overwhelmingly of a certain size (U.S. size two and over five feet, eight inches tall). It is a show about models and modeling potential, but there is an aspect of the show that tries to highlight that difference is beautiful. Race, ethnicity, gender, and sexuality are all aspects that producers highlight and explore in each cycle. The panel of judges asks the competing women to embrace and feature what makes them different and unique. But, in the end, this is a show based on physical appearance and many women are asked to be thin and conventionally or commercially attractive in order to gain access to modeling contracts and campaigns for clients such as Sephora and Cover Girl cosmetics. The show holds in tension notions of embracing one's looks and embracing the standards of the fashion industry.

The bodies portrayed on *ANTM* can both reproduce and subvert traditional understandings of beauty and what is a beautiful body. The contestants chosen to compete can help to deconstruct conventional understandings of attractive bodies and what consumers want to see advertised (similar to the Dove "Real Beauty" campaign) or they can concretize the fetishization of a certain type of beauty that is unattainable for the overwhelming majority of people.

Bodies in Motion

So You Think You Can Dance airs on the FOX network in the United States. During the televised audition process, a variety of amateur and professional dancers takes the stage and perform in front of the cameras, an audience of other dancers, and a panel of judges. The panel of judges critiques the dancers after a ninety-second audition. The styles of dance range from ballet to animation. Some are contemporary, others b-boys and b-girls. A few perform "free style," which is often a signal on the show that the dancer is not trained professionally nor do they have much experience.

The panel frequently snickers at those that do not have a typical dancer's body (strong, slender, graceful). While the mockery is not overt, it still happens. More often than not, the head judge and executive producer, Nigel Lythgoe, informs the dancer that they are not right for the competition because of their weight, citing lack of stamina, or he states that their weight will be an issue in partnering—a key component of the show.

There are those who seek negative attention. Some potential contestants audition outfitted as birds. Some audition in lingerie. Others stray from the conventional dance attire and wear outfits that would seem more in place on a dominatrix than someone auditioning for a primetime dance show aimed at families.

The next step in the process to "making it to the live shows" happens when dancers partner together in callbacks, called "Vegas Week." During this week, they try out different styles of dance like jazz, hip-hop, and contemporary. The top twenty dancers that finally make it to the live shows have jumped through many hoops to be there, and not only are their dance abilities weighed in the cut, but so are their personalities. The eventual winner is chosen by viewer votes.

Supposedly being telegenic is not part of the decision process in making it to the Top Twenty, but there are few unattractive contestants. Most would be considered conventionally attractive. Some even board what judge Mary Murphy calls the "Hot Tamale Train." To be aboard the train means that you have just danced in an exciting, engaging manner.

The contestants on the live shows are dressed in elaborate costumes and the dance routines often require props. For instance, in season ten a woman was entangled in ropes throughout much of the number, her arms strung up like a marionette. Dancers throughout the seasons have danced on tables, beds, benches, couches, and on set pieces made to resemble jail bars.

The choreography pushes the dancers' bodies in new ways. They have to try jazz one week and Bollywood the next, then hip hop followed by contemporary. They may have only had professional training in one style and the choreographers often seem to have a sadistic glint in their eyes when debuting the choreography to the dancers. "Punishing," "difficult," and "nonstop" are often bandied about when describing the routines to the audience. The dancers have only a few days to learn at least two routines. The closer a dancer gets to the finale, the more dances they have to learn that week.

Sometimes they get hurt. Bodies give out. Muscles get sprained, bones break, ligaments tear. These are all common occurrences in dancers, but many times, they continue to dance. Pain and discomfort will not stop them. After all, the show must go on. Their bodies may be broken or hurt in some manner, but training and bodily discipline compels the dancers to continue.

These descriptions of *So You Think You Can Dance* tell us a lot about televisual bodies in motion. First, the body is usually young (the upper age limit is twenty-nine), beautiful, and lithe. There are many critiques to be launched against the body types that are preferred, including that programs like this promote only a certain standard of beauty. Race is important to note here. The dancers have various racial and ethnic backgrounds and race is often not mentioned. One example that counters this happened in season ten. When critiquing a male African American dancer's performance of an Afro Jazz routine, the executive producer, Nigel Lythgoe, stated: "People say, 'This is your ethnicity, your heritage.' But it isn't! You didn't grow up in a jungle!" This occurrence stands out as one of the few times that race was used as a social marker in this show.

Second, the body is often pushed to extremes. Whether mastering a new dance style or learning extremely difficult choreography, the dancers' bodies contort and form new shapes. Their geographies are unusual. The contours of the body shift, as does the music. The body tells a story in these dances. But I have to harken back to the size and shape of the bodies. These slim and fit bodies tell a story in unscripted TV as well. They show that an overweight body doesn't fit into televised portrayals of bodies in motion. We, as a society, are not used to seeing fat jiggle and big butts wiggle on TV. Even though American society has significant obesity issues, we still prefer to see slim bodies on our televisions. We are socially and visually conditioned to see slender bodies as graceful and overweight bodies as unsightly.

Body Norms

Analysis of the geography of bodies and of portrayals of those bodies on television provides a situation in which society and culture can be analyzed as well. Whether the bodies are confined bodies, "model" bodies, or bodies in motion, they represent social constructions and norms. The bodily geographies of reality television can open up spaces of dialogue regarding norms of bodies and whose bodies are portrayed. While there is a high degree of homogeneity among the competitors on these programs, media scholars and feminists argue that differences in bodies are imperative to show on television because of the lack of diversity currently and historically in television programming. Although television is more diverse now, it is still overwhelmingly of a certain demographic structure. Unscripted television is changing the demographics of television.

Television is central in the dissemination of cultural and spatial ideologies. We learn acceptable behaviors and/or language from this medium. We learn new styles of fashion and music. We learn what is socially constructed as beautiful and what is not. We learn definitions of public and private spaces. We learn how to maneuver those public and private spaces and what actions are normal in each space.

The porous boundaries of public and private spaces become visible in the study of unscripted television. Public and private spaces collide when "private" parts become public viewing material and then infiltrate the private home. There is a blurring of the divide between private acts and public space when something that is theoretically meant for private consumption becomes part of a public identity.

The public privates portrayed in reality/unscripted television show how media can influence understanding of social mores. Social norms are shifting as media is increasingly infiltrating society. As a society, television, including unscripted television, is changing how we view each other and ourselves. What this means is that we are at a time in our culture today where we can reevaluate social standards regarding what is "reel" and what is "real." As media changes, our conceptions and perceptions of space and place change as well. Socio-spatial codings portrayed within media influence how the audience understands the reel/real relationship.

7

Kinky Geographies

Sexuality in Mediated Spaces

In this chapter, I look at two very specific media—the fetish magazine *Bizarre* and the online blog of sex activist Kitty Stryker—in order to discuss the social geographies formed by each and the relationships between sexuality, the body, and mediated spaces. These two media are linked through the promotion of kink and the formation of a "community of kink." Kitty Stryker spreads positive messages of sex and her blog will be juxtaposed with the fetish focus of *Bizarre* and the community of kink it creates. The two case studies allow us to examine how sexuality is explored and portrayed in print and virtual media, as well as to investigate erotica as a geographical concern.

Erotica is a complicated subject. It is not a static concept, but it is often treated as if it were. For the purposes of this book, erotica refers to the sexualized images or descriptions promoted in print and various other media. Writing about erotica can be problematic for a feminist geographer since erotica has been a hotly debated issue for feminists for decades.[1]

Although discussion over the issue has waxed and waned over time, the subject remains sensitive. With the explosion of the Internet in the 1990s, erotica was brought again to the forefront of feminist debates.

Three feminist positions on erotica are usually expressed in these debates: "anti-pornography," "liberal," or "pro-sex." Anti-pornography feminists have framed erotica through domination discourses. They argue that gender oppression is achieved through a sexuality that caters to "male" appetites and desires.[2] Anti-pornography feminists see women's bodies as commodified and exploited. Liberal feminists see erotica as a free speech issue, combining that right with a woman's right to use her own body as she pleases.[3] Pro-sex feminists have claimed that alternative sexual practices and feminism should go hand in hand.[4] They also challenge the idea that erotica reflects simply a male desire and they argue that "women *do* look."[5]

A geographic perspective on erotica adds an important element to current debates. Erotica is important to study precisely because of the issues wrapped up in the politics of representation of society. Yet erotica is a subject rarely broached by geographers, feminist or otherwise.[6] Williams argues, "Mainstream or margin, erotica is emphatically part of American culture."[7] Erotica is still treated as a taboo subject in academia, although the use of erotic images is growing every day due to the expansion of the Internet.

Media geography provides an interesting backdrop to examinations of erotica and the body since there are no "real" bodies in media, only portrayals of bodies. In addition, there is a collision of public and private in the world of erotica. There is a move from the private space of the bedroom to the public/private space of the mediated spaces.[8] According to Bronski, "The explosion of private sexual fantasy into public view is a powerful political statement."[9] The collision between public and private has traditionally been a subject for geographers, so it is remarkable that mediated erotica has remained marginalized, even stigmatized, as a subject of study.

Bizarre

This section examines a particular genre of sexuality—fetishes—through analysis of John Willie's magazine, *Bizarre*. *Bizarre* centered on Willie's photographs and illustrations as well as a correspondence section that featured letters and photographs from readers. Topics included BDSM (bondage and discipline, domination and submission, sadism and masochism), cross-dressing, extreme fashion, and body modification (such as tattoos and piercing). While the magazine has been read as an ironic commentary on gender, this section critically engages the imagery promoted in *Bizarre*'s volumes through two geographies—a geography which centers at the nexus of the body and dress and a geography of a fetish community.

When I first encountered John Willie, it was in a dark, dusty bookstore in Seattle. The thick volumes of *Bizarre* stood out on the bookshelf. I took them down and perused though them, paid twenty bucks for my purchase, and then promptly forgot about them for nearly twenty years. After unpacking some boxes that had been sitting in my basement for years, I rediscovered the evocative books in their shiny (well, now dirty) black cover. This is where this chapter begins.

John Willie (aka John Alexander Scott Coutts) was a pioneer in fetish fashion and bondage illustration and photography. He published the aforementioned fetish fashion magazine, *Bizarre*, from 1946 to 1959. The introduction to the reprint of *Bizarre* calls him the "Leonardo da Vinci of Fetish."[10] Others refer to him as the "Rembrandt of Pulp."[11] Willie hoped his magazine would appeal to readers with a mixture of the pulp format of the Hollywood celebrity magazine, strip cartoons, and humor.[12] Willie was considered a purveyor of "sleazy-porn"—dangerous and corrupt in the strict moral codes of the 1950s United States. Although deemed as such, *Bizarre* did not follow the conventions of erotica (there are no explicit and graphic sexual acts).[13] Willie was careful in his negotiation of obscenity laws in the United States, using coded language and "avoiding nudity, homosexuality, overt violence or obvious depictions of things that might be read as perverse or immoral and that might rankle those parties who were capable of banning, censoring or blocking circulation."[14]

Likely drawing its name from *Harper's Bazaar*, America's first women's fashion magazine, *Bizarre* had a circulation of "5,000 solid citizens" from England, New Zealand, Australia, Canada, and the United States.[15] The magazine was distributed via the mail to those who paid the subscription fee to Willie. It was not available in any retail establishments. Willie's

Bizarre featured pictures of women being bound and constricted, and it sexualized their immobility to his readers and future generations. Over fifty years later, his illustrations are still prominently featured online.

Willie, a proponent of "consensual bondage," focused primarily on women's bodies in his work, but danced with gender stereotypes at times.[16] He avoided discussion of homosexuality, although readers discussed gendered performances and transgressions in correspondence sections. Although gender was sometimes constructed as fluid, Willie always emphasized heteronormativity in his captions to illustrations or in articles accompanying pictures.[17]

Bizarre's depictions of models bound and gagged in fetish apparel and lingerie were seen as taboo, racy, and extreme for the 1940s and 1950s, but in hindsight, they were relatively tame compared to magazines published now. The fashion to be found in *Bizarre* differs little from that shown today. In Valerie Steele's discussion of fantasy, fetish, and fashion, she wrote, "Today bondage, leather, rubber, 'second skins,' long, tight skirts, split dresses, zipped bottines—everything from a fetishist's dream—is available directly from Alai'a, Gaultier, Montana, Versace."[18] As *Vogue* magazine reported, many of the world's most important fashion designers were inspired by sexual "perversity."[19] Nowadays, fashion and lifestyle magazines feature over-the-knee, sky-high heeled boots on a regular basis. Celebrities on the red carpet and models on the runway wear heels that teeter over five inches tall (as do people who are not celebrities and models). Pencil skirts are also currently en vogue, albeit they are not the extreme hobble skirts as shown in *Bizarre*.

Confining Clothes, Sexual Liberation

Michel Foucault described sexuality in the United States of the mid-twentieth century as confined unless it was "utilitarian and fertile."[20] For Willie, *Bizarre* was sexually liberating for him and his readers: "It has no particular sense, rhyme, nor reason, but typifies that freedom for which we fought . . . the freedom to say what we like, wear what we like, and to amuse ourselves as we like in our own sweet way."[21] How they amused themselves was mostly through images of fetish fashion.

A fetish, in the most basic of terms, is arousal stimulated by a particular object or situation. Body types and races are fetishized as are articles of clothing, body parts, and so on. Foucault described "fetishism" as "the model perversion," which "served as the guiding thread for analyzing all the other deviations."[22] Rejecting the psychoanalytic view of sexuality, Foucault instead argued that the "psychiatrization of perverse pleasure" was the modern equivalent of the confessional and the latest form of knowledge-power subverting the essentialism/constructivism binary.[23] For Anne Hamlyn, a "fetish is tacitly understood as something compulsive, an unthinking and self-indulgent erotic . . . foible associated with the unmastered body and the so-called primitive."[24] Yet, as Julia Pine writes, "the pathologization of fetishism did not surface in the pages of *Bizarre*. In fact, *Bizarre* can be read very much as an antidote to the vilification and classification of fetishism as perversions; instead, it was a space for the naturalization of kinkiness. . . . In *Bizarre* the overall impression is one of a neutral space or 'safe zone'—a refuge or gathering place for those whose ritual and preferences were labeled elsewhere as perversions [or] paraphilias."[25] *Bizarre* created a safe space for those who were so inclined to explore alternative aspects of their sexuality through fetish fashion imagery.

Fashion is important to understand as it is a social and individual act. Dress is an embodied experience. Joanne Entwistle, as cited by Anna Secor, argues that "the study of dress as situated practice requires moving between, on the one hand, the discursive and representational aspects of dress, and the way the body/dress is caught up in relations of power, and on the other, the embodied experience of dress and the use of dress as a means by which individuals orientate themselves to the social world."[26]

Dress is one link between the body and mobility. For Anna Secor, "any 'reading' of dress must take into account its corporeality, the link with the body that confers upon dress the critical dimension of mobility."[27] The relationship between bodies, dress, and mobility show how certain dress of the body can restrict or enable movement.

Valerie Steele writes that for "masochists, even a moderately laced corset has a marvelously negative effect on the mobility, balance, and physical stability of its wearer."[28] Jones relates it to sexual attraction: "Men do like high heels for the constricting effect they give to the female walk."[29] Steele quotes designer Vivienne Westwood: "The bondage clothes were ostensibly restrictive, but when you put them on they gave you a feeling of freedom."[30]

Fetish fashion has been commonplace and sold commercially for decades. All issues of *Bizarre* feature corseting, while the second most popular fetish gear portrayed was black boots. Quoting a rubber enthusiast, Steele writes: "The 1960s were wonderful years for those of us interested in exotic-erotic wear."[31] In fact, kinky boots, leather, and corset-style lacing were even being sold at department stores like Montgomery Ward(!) in the early 1970s.

Additionally, *Bizarre* advertised mail-order shoes (with a minimum six-inch heel). Steele argues that evidence exists of correlations between Western high-heeled shoes and foot-binding: "Western high-heeled shoes, which give the visual illusion of smaller feet and produces a swaying walk may be derived from foot-binding."[32] Steele continues by discussing how extreme high heels constrict the wearer's movements and how that can be construed as erotic. There are, of course, many who argue that high heels are as repressive as corsets and just as dangerous to the body, but there are just as many (regardless of gender) who enjoy wearing high heels (or corsets for that matter) for myriad reasons.

Willie also framed the magazine as an outlet for extreme fashions in order to avoid censorship.[33] Coded as such, *Bizarre* looks like a girly magazine focused on women's fashion, but to those who were in the know (those in the fetish subculture), it provided "a safe virtual space in which those with 'alternative' sexual tastes and a preference for unconventional gender performance could meet and commune."[34] Gender fluidity was part of the appeal of the magazine, as can be deduced from the correspondence section, and the magazine often featured tips for cross-dressers.[35]

Bizarre Justifications

Bondage imagery was sometimes coded as a fashion faux pas or as "figure training." For example, a woman bound in a single glove behind her back was captioned with "Single Glove to prevent slouching and stooping," and women were warned to not be too alluring to others: "Lady beware!

Don't make yourself too pretty for the party! The boy friend may decide it's not safe to let you go out!"[36]

The murder of two of Willie's models shed negative light on the publication of *Bizarre*. One of them fell victim to Henry Glatman— called the "Bondage Murderer," "Glamour Girl Slayer," or "Lonely-Hearts Killer"— who was active during the time of *Bizarre*'s publication. He was a rapist in addition to being murderer. As a teenager, he would break into women's apartments, tie them up, rape them, and take pictures as souvenirs. As an adult, he hired women for modeling work, tied them up, sexually assaulted them, and then strangled them. For these acts, he also kept pictures as mementos.

Often *Bizarre* implied that the women bound and gagged on its pages were victims of kidnapping or burglary and advised women to not let themselves fall prey to intruders. In every issue, Willie couched his magazine as an advocate for self-defense. His images had captions that read: "Don't let this happen to you. Learn jiu-jitsu, the art of self-defense."[37]

Kitty Stryker: Kink Activist

According to her blog (kittystryker.com), Kitty Stryker is a writer, activist, performer, sexpert, queer femme, and cat mom.[38] She writes on topics such as sex work, gender, sexuality, patriarchy, feminism, body image, and obscenity. Kitty cofounded the "artsy sexy party" Kinky Salon London, the Ladies High Tea and Pornography Society, and the San Francisco–based kink party Whippersnappers. Her blog is the focus of this case study as it covers a number of topics connected to *Bizarre*—namely, that of "deviant" sexualities and communities of kink.

Kitty Stryker's discussion of sex and sexuality is open and blunt. She often uses her own experiences in her blogs to frame her sex activism.

> It used to be that when I asked for something kinky it was because the sex we were having bored me. I fetishize novelty, and I've been in these communities for 14 years. It's difficult to come up with something new and exciting for this jaded libido! So I would enjoy the vanilla sex for a while, then we'd get into spanking or toys or role plays because the sex

on its own wasn't enough to hold my interest anymore. Developing a power exchange was not about trust or intimacy so much as it was about creating a distraction. Not so this time. I realized that I wanted him to cuff me because I trusted him enough to be willing to see what he'd do if I was immobilized. I wanted to tell him what my fantasies were, the silly ones and the dark ones. This time it was about a deepening of intimacy, not a deflection. It wasn't about submission, or pain, but surrendering—not to him, but to my own desires. I have always been both incredibly open about sex and very shielded about some of my own fantasies, but I have had nothing to fear from him. He has never laughed at me, never once made me feel self-conscious. He caresses my belly, my upper arms, my thighs and I feel beautiful.[39]

Her experiences color all of her blogs and Stryker is comfortable exploring different aspects of her sexuality and sexual activities with her readers. The ways she confronts social constructions of sexuality are important to note. Her discussions of power relations in sex often highlight how gender relations play out sexually. One example is when she describes wrapping her male partner in cling film and immobilizing him. Her visceral reaction to his immobility is an aphrodisiac to her and she finds her desire increasing to the point of feeling an animalistic blood lust.

Stryker fully discusses her thoughts on kinky geographies and how they affect behaviors in public and private spaces. Her writing is an example of public privates because she often uses her framings of public and private spaces to examine how sexuality and kink are portrayed in both media and "real" life.

Stryker, in a blog entry discussing BDSM in movies such as *Fifty Shades of Grey* and *Secretary*, refutes the idea that "people into kink are messed up."[40] Regarding *Secretary*'s suggestion that BDSM may be rooted in self-harm, she argues that "a lot of people have been touched by abuse, whether kinky or not, and while self-harm isn't a path to kink, it can be for some."[41] Stryker goes on to discuss how BDSM is done a disservice when it is portrayed as abusive in nature.

Stryker often explores representations of dominants in popular media, both male and female. Her interest lies in her work as a professional dominatrix (ProDomme). Here she describes prominent depictions of female dominants:

> Almost always in heels and latex, slender and young and beautiful. If they're lucky, they get to be smart, though often never as smart as the male romantic lead (of which there is always one), and ultimately they desire to be overpowered and outsmarted by said male lead. And usually they're professionals, because obviously women aren't interested in kinky sex by themselves, they need a guy to persuade them in either case. Female dominants are depicted as bored, cold, mentally ill, only in it for the money, laughable, or some combination of the above . . . and the men they dominate are not seen as romantic possibilities, but pathetic. Their cries for their limits to be respected are the punch line of a joke, or meant to be humiliating.[42]

In her discussion of dominance and gender relations, Stryker explores how gender follows traditionally patriarchal roles in many media depictions. These manifestations of patriarchy in sexuality are often juxtaposed in her blog with ways to subvert traditional sex roles of the "active" male and "passive" female.

While sex and kink positive, Stryker does explore aspects of the fetish community with which she is uncomfortable. Discussing Adult Baby/ Diaper Lovers (AB/DL), she states: "I've had my own struggles with it as a kink and finding acceptance around it. I think that it's generally pretty easy to turn away if someone is engaging in a kinky activity that doesn't do it for you, so I don't see why kinksters don't do more of that instead of being so scornful. As for the media, well, the sooner everyone realizes that most media around sex is only there to be sensational and shocking, not educational, and create their sound bytes accordingly, the better I say."[43] It is interesting to note here that the fetish and kink community is not monolithic and has factions within it. When Stryker describes AB/ DL, she expresses a tolerance of it even though it doesn't "do it for [her]." Her analysis of media in her blog shows a reel/real division that can create even more divides in the fetish community.

Further on in the post, she describes a distinct geography of kink and frames it in terms of my argument of public privates:

> My kinks are not something that need to be explored in all/any public settings. Context is important here. . . . I don't know that I would argue that M/s [Master/slave] relationships have a "right" to use collars and leashes in public, either, or that human puppies "should" be allowed to run around in kit at a dog park. While I will certainly fight for consenting adults to have the right to do as they like in private, I do also feel that all public space is not an appropriate place for sexual behaviour. People have a right to not be in sexualized space when they haven't sought it out—never mind the fact that sexual energy can be triggering for people. I've done a lot of public play, but it's either been pretty subtle or explainable, or it's been empty of other people. I think it'd be amazing if there were more spaces where you can enjoy public kink, same as I like having spaces to enjoy public sex. . . . I love Folsom and Dore [a BDSM and leather fetish event], where public kink and sex are fairly common. But they're restricted spaces—entry means consenting to being around sex and kink. I mean, I live in SF, where, to be honest, you can probably do many kinky things in public under the guise of public performance and keep it playful without any issues. I think that's awesome, and that's why I live here. There is a social agreement that makes a lot of stuff ok. But there *is* a line, and I'm ok with that.[44]

The geographies that Stryker discusses are fundamental to understanding how gendered and patriarchal notions of sex and sexuality are constructed in today's society. It is simultaneously a debunking and an endorsement of the "behind closed doors" philosophy. Propriety is central to her mental mapping and geographical understandings of public and private spaces. There is a distinct sense of social boundaries when she blogs about public space.

She continues her geographical discussion through an examination of gender, sexuality, and privilege: "I also rarely see female public sex at these various kink/sex in public type places, certainly not as often as men. . . . If I engage in sexual behaviour with another woman at Folsom, say, the likelihood that men will try to physically involve themselves with my scene is a lot greater. So, it's a double-edged sword, this 'freedom' I have. It's a freedom that comes, often, with a price of dealing with male entitlement."[45] Public sexuality and how it affects women is something she sees as an important social issue. It feeds into the argument of public privates as it takes something typically private or intimate and puts it in the public arena.

Stryker writes on her take on sex, kink, and patriarchy often. By doing that, she highlights societal constructs of propriety. This is important to discuss as many of those who partake in kink are "closeted" to some degree. The closeting of kink can be isolating for some, but it can also lead to a desire for community, for a connection with those who have the same interests.

Community of Kink

Readers of *Bizarre* and those who follow the lifestyles described in Stryker's blog can be seen as part of an "imagined community" of kink.[46] In his work on imagined communities, Benedict Anderson discusses how media can cement certain behaviors and identities.[47] Participants in communities of kink become united by their fetishes or desires. These communities are not, however, always considered inclusionary or positive. Stryker's and *Bizarre*'s communities of kink are described quite differently.

The idea of community surfaces repeatedly in Stryker's blogs, but not always in a positive way. Here she tells a story of being excluded from an event:

> Just in case I was feeling overly confident about where I stand in the BDSM "community," I found myself on the receiving end of event expulsion thanks to an ex of mine. . . . The construct of "community" is one I question a lot being placed on BDSM groupings, because I don't believe we are one simply because we like the same toys. To me, community indicates some agreements to a standard of behaviour, and accountability/responsibility to each other for following that code of conduct. If those things are not in place, actively and, again, transparently, I question how much of a community it is. Granted, I not only question the use of the word "community," I also question our leadership—who

becomes a leader and why. I find over and over again that it's the (often self-appointed) "community leaders" who I get the most reports about when it comes to overstepping boundaries.[48]

Here again, we see that the kink community is not a singular experience for those enmeshed in it. There is also a policing of the community as mentioned by the overstepping of boundaries. Decisions regarding this policing affect the inclusionary/exclusionary politics of communities of kink.

The correspondence section of *Bizarre* created a community of fetishists or enthusiasts, as some prefer to be called (since the term "fetish" is laden with moral codes and connotes perversion). Readers could realize they weren't alone in their proclivities. McClintock describes private, ritualized spaces of kink "as the secret society of the spectacle."[49] One reader wrote: "Dear Sir . . . Since my wife has been reading *Bizarre* she has realized my interests are not so strange and that others do likewise. Thanks to you Mr. Editor I can now dress as I please on occasion. As a corset lover this means high heels and real original wasp-waisted corsets to give a five or six inch reduction in waist measure."[50] Readers sent in photographs of themselves or partners in costumes or fetish gear, including extreme shoes and boots and extremely tight outfits. Humor was widely employed as a device to play down the sexual aspects of the photographs.

Willie was upset that he could not cater to every fetish in every issue. In issue two, Willie wrote, "It takes all sorts to make this world, and it is a bit of a task to please everyone, but we will do our best, taking it in turns."[51] He attempted to please all with Miss Bizarre (featured in issue eleven). Miss Bizarre signified the popular fetishes of *Bizarre*'s readers. She was meant to be an amalgamation of reader preferences. To gratify his audience, he crammed a number of fetishes into one illustration: high heels, hobble skirts, bondage, and blindfolding.

The community to which *Bizarre* readers belonged is important because they saw it as inclusionary. It allowed readers to explore aspects of their sexuality and sexual proclivities without admonishment or judgment. It was a way that their clandestine fantasies could become a public expression.

These communities of kink, as I call them, are often founded on similarities, but as Stryker reveals that can be insufficient to create unity and inclusion. Deviance from and transgression of traditional sexuality may not be enough on which to base a community.

Deviance and Transgression

Bizarre fetishized many aspects of dress and the body. This section examines only a few. On *Bizarre*'s pages, the body was restricted in many ways, whether through fashion or bondage. Many of those that engage in the bondage lifestyle consider the constricting gear and attire liberating for their sexuality as evidenced by the letters in the correspondence section. The restriction of the body though fetish fashion or through bondage freed many of *Bizarre*'s readers to pursue their fantasies.

The normalization of deviance and gender/body transgression in *Bizarre* was an anomaly at the time in which it was published. Strict moral codes surrounding sex and the body abounded then and still appear today. While many would argue that moral codes of conduct are more relaxed today, we can turn to a number of situations in the United States and around the world where specific ideas of normalcy and acceptability are superimposed onto others' bodies.

Stryker continues the exploration of patriarchal constructions of sexuality as she recounts her work as a ProDomme and her encounters with female dominance and male submission. She also details her disgust for arrogant male dominants who seek to make her submissive or question her skills as a female dominant. Her discussions of patriarchal standards and often "toxic" masculinity demonstrate that she is attuned to a feminist understanding of socio-spatial interactions.

Stryker's work to upend patriarchy extends to another undertaking of hers. In Stryker's Andro-Aperture Project, she seeks to disrupt traditional conceptions of male beauty and attractiveness. Stryker embraces transgression and transgressive bodies. In her activism, she seeks to unsettle patriarchal constraints on sexuality and beauty for everyone (regardless of gender). She is resolute in her efforts to normalize all forms of sex, sexuality, and bodies. The Andro-Aperture Project is "a project about the female gaze and erotic male nudes."[52] Stryker is crusading for appreciation of and respect for male bodies in all forms. For her and those who work on the project, "We believe increasing the quantity and availability of imagery of the sexualized male body, particularly beyond a gay context, increases social acceptance of these otherwise transgressive expressions."[53]

Kinky Geographies

Both *Bizarre* and Stryker's work show mediated geographies that play with notions of gender, sexuality, and erotica in a number of different ways. Media opens up a space for involvement in kinky geographies. Media can help to create an interactive community—inclusionary or not. Communities of kink, acceptable acts in space, and conceptions of bodies are topics explored in the two case studies. While quite different forms of media, they depict two similar understandings of how kink should be embraced through its representation in print and virtually mediated spaces.

The mediation of kink that occurs in both cases depicts geographies of public and private space. Kink becomes an act of public privates. The collision of public and private spaces becomes evident in both *Bizarre's* pages and Stryker's blog. An examination of kinky geographies demonstrates how public privates are constructed with regard to sex and sexuality. Constructions of sex and sexuality by society reveal much about how patriarchy is upheld or subverted. By allowing kink to become more public in a positive way, affirmative portrayals have the potential to destigmatize kink and to liberate those who are closeted.

8

Public Privates Exposed
Media, Gender, and Space

In this book I have explored how the concept of "public privates" is portrayed across various media. By understanding how geographies are produced through private acts in public (mediated) spaces, gendered norms and stereotypes are placed under scrutiny. Examination of visual media leads to examination of public and private spaces and how those spaces affect everyday geographies of viewers. I have argued that depictions of behaviors in the media examined here led to both reification and destabilization of gendered geographies of public and private spaces. These case studies show the blurred boundaries between public and private spaces and demonstrate the notion of "public privates" through analysis of gendered identities in visual media. Mediated public and private spaces influence constructed distinctions between actual public and private spaces.

"Welcome to the Hellmouth: Paradoxical Spaces in *Buffy the Vampire Slayer*" examined geographies of fear depicted in public and private spaces. Monsters attack Sunnydale daily (and nightly). Public spaces become places to be feared; yet there are also places to be reclaimed as refuges. Teenage Buffy rules the streets, which have traditionally been gendered as masculine spaces. Private spaces, including the home and body, are also shown paradoxically. The home is both a haven and a site of violence. When vampires or other creatures invade the home, the safety and sanctity of the home is breached and fear occurs. The home is often gendered as a feminine space, but it is also open to violation. Intrusions of private space, whether home or body, can create geographies of fear within the home. These fears are also manifested in public spaces.

As seen in the chapter "Home Is Where the Heart Is: *Fast and Furious* Geographies," the concepts of family and home are central to the *Fast and Furious* series. While territoriality and a sense of equality in the streets are also present in the franchise, the films center on a constructed family and their desire to be together no matter what challenges they may confront. Villains, state authorities, prison, and amnesia separate the crew, but they always find a way back home. The family is drawn together not only by bloodlines, but a common love of racing. The actions scenes propel the series, but the heart of the franchise is the family.

The gendering of behaviors and actions in the *Fast and Furious* films is also important to examine because of the potential to disrupt patriarchal norms. Certain norms are upheld in the films through the stereotypically brawny male characters, but others are destabilized through portrayal and development of the female characters. Characters such as Hobbs and Dom represent the hypermasculine, and Letty is musculinized, but other feminist elements—harkening back to the notion of equality throughout the franchise—can subvert traditional stereotypes of female characters. There are no damsels in distress, but instead extremely skilled women who hold their own.

J-Horror films are analyzed in "Scared to Death: Spaces of J-Horror." These films show how evil penetrates private spaces including the home and the body (sometimes literally). The supernatural interrupts the balance between good/evil and living/dead. J-Horror portrays the permeability of bodies and homes.

When the body or home are invaded, horror occurs. Transgression of boundaries triggers feeling of abjection and terror. *Ringu*, *Dark Water*, *Audition*, and *The Grudge* all depict examples of horrific geographies. Terror is elicited when ghosts and monsters (human or otherwise) become real and infiltrate the most intimate and private realms. This idea is central to understanding how terror works in both the reel and real worlds because it reveals much about socio-spatial relations and our understandings of public and private spaces.

In "Visions of Gender: Codings of Televisual Space," examination of the homes and workplaces of classic twentieth-century television programs show how roles of Mother, Father, and Working Woman affect and code public and private spaces. Popular twentieth-century sitcoms such as *Roseanne*, *The Cosby Show*, *The Mary Tyler Moore Show*, and *Murphy Brown* highlighted the role of television in gendering (re)production. As shown through portrayals of Mother and Father, the home becomes both a refuge and a burden, while understandings of Working Woman masculinize the workplace. Private space is exemplified in the home and the workplace is considered public. Reification of gendered norms regarding home and work, and thus (re)production, happens as certain characteristics are valued in each space.

Public space is the primary setting for Degrassi Community School, the case study for "Navigating Degrassi Community School: Socio-Spatial Identities in *Degrassi*." Within the school setting, students interact in a variety of ways. These exchanges help to form their teenage identities and the way they formulate their mental maps and geographical imaginations. *Degrassi* highlights and portrays many issues that teen viewers face in their real lives. The body geographies the series depicts center on disclosure of identity, sexual assault, and violence/death. Because these are realities for many teens, it is important that the show portrays them as genuinely as possible and treats its characters and viewers with respect. I argue that *Degrassi* deals with the stories it tells in a responsible manner that supports its audience in times of crisis.

"Big Brother Is Watching You: Why You Should Be Watching Reality TV" examines reality or "unscripted" television. Reality shows such as *Big Brother*, *America's Next Top Model*, and *So You Think You Can Dance* all show private acts in a public way. Three types of bodies are analyzed: the confined body, the "model" body, and the body in motion. These categories show the bias of reality programming, while also highlighting how different bodies are depicted on television. The way that the private now overlaps with the public demonstrates the manifestation of social relations in televised spaces. Within the programs chosen for analysis, porosity between and fragility of constructions of public and private spaces are illustrated and exemplified.

In "Kinky Geographies: Sexuality in Mediated Spaces," I concentrated on sexualized bodies in two print media forms—the blog of sex activist Kitty Stryker and the fetish magazine *Bizarre*. The representations and images in these media have real effects, which influence socio-spatial understandings. Stryker's blog examines sexual mores and "deviant" sexual behaviors in an autobiographical narrative. John Willie's print magazine, *Bizarre*, portrayed fetish wear and was built on materials from readers— primarily photographs and letters. Both media exemplify ways in which a community of kink can be created. Geographical understandings of sexuality in these instances inform notions of transgression and deviance and how they play out in public and private spaces.

Throughout this discussion, mediated space links the chapters and forms the argument that public and private spaces are intrinsically bound to one another. Perceived barriers blend, yet on the other hand, mediated spaces can work to uphold those same barriers. Public and private spaces need each other to exist in an interdependent relationship. Examples of bodies, homes, workplaces, schools, and streets demonstrate how one cannot fully understand public and private space as exclusive elements.

Visual media can erode constructed divisions between public and private spaces and form "public privates." This notion of the dissolution of barriers between public and private space can be a liberating ideology in which patriarchal understandings are overturned. Yet visual media can also concretize those divides and create an unequal dualism of public/private in which the public is considered dominant and preferred over the private.

We have seen how media images affect mental maps and geographical imaginations of public and private space and influence how society interacts. Media coding of spaces tells viewers how to act in particular settings, how to interact with others, and how to formulate one's own identity. Gendered codings shape gender relations and identities. They often teach patriarchal understandings of masculinity and femininity that can be detrimental to social relations. There is also the possibility of a liberating text that shakes off the traditional notions surrounding gender and gendered behaviors.

Media help to shape our daily experiences and perceptions of the world around us. They inform our geographical imaginations and create mental maps of both reel and real spaces and places. Media work to create illustrations of the world around us. Sometimes these portrayals are based in real events and others based in fantasy. No matter the root of the depiction, media have the potential to change how we interact with the spaces we encounter every day. It is important to reflect on how we conceptualize space and how those conceptualizations are mediated. The reel/real binary discussed in this book has the power to influence socio-spatial relations on a number of levels.

Future Directions

Media are omnipresent in many lives. Media images and sounds permeate interactions every day. The bombardment of media that many of us experience in large amounts influences our negotiations of both people and places. As media change and infiltrate more and more aspects of daily life, examination of the messages transmitted is more important than at any time prior.

The mobile aspect of media and how this new flexibility affects understandings and normings of public and private spaces will become ever more important as it penetrates more and more facets of daily life. Mobile media change our geographical imaginations and mental mappings of the world around us. Our involvement with mobile media can create a disruption of the reel/real binary.

When the reel and real blur together, they create public privates. Public space and private space become further intertwined and, therefore, they require further inquiry into the effects of that imbrication.

As media continually inform constructions of public and private spaces, they form new geographies. These include geographies of home, work, community, and bodies.

These new spaces open up moments of potential destabilization for patriarchal formulations of gender identity and normed behaviors. It is critical that gender and media scholars examine the effects of media on the social conditioning of people and places. Through an investigation of popular media, new understandings of socio-spatial relationships are uncovered.

TV

America's Next Top Model (2003–)

Big Brother (2000–)

Buffy the Vampire Slayer
(1997–2003)

Degrassi (2001–2015)

Leave it to Beaver (1957–1963)

Murphy Brown (1988–1998)

Roseanne (1988–1997)

So You Think You Can Dance
(2005–)

The Cosby Show (1984–1992)

The Mary Tyler Moore Show
(1970–1977)

The Real World (1992–)

Movies

2 Fast 2 Furious (2003)

Audition (1999)

Dark Water (2002)

Dark Water (2005)

The Fast and the Furious (2001)

Fast & Furious (2009)

Fast & Furious 6 (2013)

*The Fast and the Furious:
Tokyo Drift* (2006)

Fast Five (2011)

Furious 7 (2015)

The Grudge (2004)

Ju-On (2002)

The Ring (2001)

Ringu (1998)

Notes

INTRODUCTION

1. Plesnar, "Represented Space in Film," 81.
2. Livingstone, "Mediated Knowledge," 100.
3. Ussher, *Fantasies of Femininity*.
4. Kellner, "Cultural Studies, Multiculturalism, and Media Culture," 5.
5. Harvey, "On the History and Present Condition of Geography"; Morley, *Television, Audiences, and Cultural Studies*; Trinta, "News from Home."
6. Hall, "Whites of Their Eyes"; Kellner, "TV, Ideology, and Emancipatory Popular Culture"; Radcliffe and Westwood, *Remaking the Nation*.
7. Hall, "Whites of Their Eyes," 18–20.
8. Gregory, *Geographical Imaginations*, 16.
9. Fiske, *Television Culture*.
10. Corner, *Critical Ideas in Television Studies*.
11. Craine, "Virtualizing Los Angeles"; Hansen, "Affect as Medium"; Levy, *Becoming Virtual*.
12. Craine, "Virtualizing Los Angeles," 235.
13. Craine, "Virtualizing Los Angeles."
14. Craine, "Virtualizing Los Angeles," 236.
15. Craine, "Virtualizing Los Angeles," 241.
16. Hansen, "Affect as Medium."
17. Hansen, "Affect as Medium," 207.
18. D'Acci, *Defining Women*; Green, *Cracks in the Pedestal*; Lee, "Subversive Sitcoms"; MacDonald, *Representing Women*; Pinedo, "Recreational Terror"; Rose, *Feminism and Geography*; Rowe, "Roseanne."
19. M. E. Brown, *Television and Women's Culture*.

20. Youngs, "English Television Landscape Documentary," 146.
21. Rose, *Feminism and Geography*; Sennett, *Flesh and Stone*.
22. Bondi and Domosh, "Contours of Public Space"; Boyer, "Place and Politics of Virtue"; Day, "Embassies and Sanctuaries"; Duncan, *BodySpace*; K. England, "Gender Relations"; Marston, "Private Goes Public"; Rose, *Feminism and Geography*; Staeheli, "Publicity, Privacy, and Women's Political Action"; Strong-Boag et al., "What Women's Spaces?"; Vaiou, "Gender Divisions in Urban Space."
23. Kaviraj, "Filth and the Public Sphere."
24. M. Douglas, *Purity and Danger*; Pile, *Body and the City*, 146.
25. Butler and Bowlby, "Bodies and Spaces"; Longhurst, "Body and Geography"; Longhurst, "(Dis)embodied Geographies"; Nast and Pile, *Places Through the Body*; Valentine, "The Body."
26. Rose, *Feminism and Geography*, 29.
27. Rose, *Feminism and Geography*, 29.
28. Livingstone, "Mediated Knowledge"; McDowell, *Gender, Identity and Place*; Meyrowitz, *No Sense of Place*; Morley, *Television, Audiences and Cultural Studies*; Thompson, "Social Theory and the Media."
29. Cresswell and Dixon, "Engaging Film," 4.
30. Fiske, *Reading the Popular*; Granello, "Using Beverly Hills, 90210"; Lindlof, *Qualitative Communication Research Methods*; Rose, *Visual Methodologies*.
31. Ardener, *Women and Space*; Bondi, "Gender, Class, and Urban Space"; Duncan, *BodySpace*; Kilian, "Public and Private"; McDowell, *Gender, Identity and Place*; Rose, *Feminism and Geography*; Spain, *Gendered Spaces*.

1. WELCOME TO THE HELLMOUTH
1. Massey, "Geographical Mind."
2. Harvey, *Social Justice and the City*; Gregory, *Geographical Imaginations*.
3. Gordon and Riger, *Female Fear*; Kern, "Selling the 'Scary City'"; Pain, "Space, Sexual Violence, and Social Control"; Rose, *Feminism and Geography*; Valentine, "London's Streets of Fear"; Valentine, "Geography of Women's Fear."
4. Kellner, "Cultural Studies," 5.
5. Duncan, *BodySpace*, 128.
6. Stanko, *Everyday Violence*; Valentine, "London's Streets of Fear"; Valentine, "Images of Danger."
7. Stanko, "Ordinary Fear," 159.
8. Gordon and Riger, *Female Fear*, 67.
9. Gerbner and Gross, "Living with Television."
10. Wilson et al., "Content Analysis of Entertainment Television."
11. Wilson et al., "Content Analysis of Entertainment Television," 16.

12. Ardener, *Women and Space*; Baumer, "Research on Fear of Crime"; Burgess, "Focusing on Fear"; Day, "Embassies and Sanctuaries"; Day, "Better Safe than Sorry?"; Gordon and Riger, *Female Fear*; Pain, "Space, Sexual Violence, and Social Control"; Smith, "Fear of Crime"; Stanko, *Everyday Violence*; Valentine, "Images of Danger"; Valentine, "London's Streets of Fear"; Valentine, "Geography of Women's Fear"; Wilson, *Sphinx in the City*.

13. Smith, "Fear of Crime"; van Dijk, "Public Attitudes toward Crime"; Warr, "Fear of Rape."

14. Wekerle and Whitzman, *Safe Cities*, 4.

15. Ardener, *Women and Space*; Day, "Constructing Masculinity"; Day, "Embassies and Sanctuaries"; Day, "Better Safe than Sorry?"; Gordon and Riger, *Female Fear*; Koskela, "Bold Walk and Breakings"; Pain, "Space, Sexual Violence, and Social Control"; Stanko, *Everyday Violence*; Valentine, "Images of Danger"; Valentine, "London's Streets of Fear"; Valentine, "Geography of Women's Fear."

16. Gordon and Riger, *Female Fear*; Stanko, "Ordinary Fear"; Valentine, "London's Streets of Fear"; Valentine, "Images of Danger"; Wekerle and Whitzman, *Safe Cities*; Wilson et al., "Content Analysis of Entertainment Television."

17. Radcliffe and Westwood, *Remaking the Nation*.

18. Radcliffe and Westwood, *Remaking the Nation*.

19. Clark Kent is the human name and alter ego of superhero Superman.

20. The Scooby Gang is the nickname of four cartoon teenagers and their dog who traveled around solving mysteries

21. Owen, "Buffy the Vampire Slayer," 28.

22. Golden and Holder, *Watcher's Guide*, 242.

23. McDowell, *Gender, Identity, and Place*, 150.

24. Koskela, "Bold Walk and Breakings," 305.

25. Tracy, *Girl's Got Bite*, 27.

26. Tasker, *Spectacular Bodies*, 149.

27. D'Acci, *Defining Women*, 3.

28. Ardener, *Women and Space*, 29.

29. Owen, "Buffy the Vampire Slayer," 25.

30. Pinedo, "Recreational Terror," 6.

31. Gelder, "Field of Horror," 3.

32. Auerbach, *Our Vampires, Ourselves*; Jarosz, "Agents of Power"; Moretti, "Capital Dracula"; Schaffer, "Wilde Desire"; Senf, "The Unseen Face."

33. M. P. Brown, *Closet Space*, 13.

34. Auerbach, *Our Vampires, Ourselves*, 145.

35. Gordon and Hollinger, "Shape of Vampires," 4.

36. Derrida, *Dissemination*.

37. Pinedo, "Recreational Terror," 21.

38. Stoker, *Dracula*, 263n1.

39. Hollinger, "Fantasies of Absence," 201.

40. Kellner, "TV, Ideology, and Emancipatory Popular Culture," 489.

41. Kellner, "TV, Ideology, and Emancipatory Popular Culture," 490.

42. Fiske, *Television Culture*, 45.

43. P. C. Adams, "Television as Gathering Place," 127.

2. HOME IS WHERE THE HEART IS

1. Jackson, "Cultural Politics of Masculinity"; Berg and Longhurst, "Placing Masculinities and Geography."

2. Corner, *Critical Ideas in Television Studies*, 88.

3. The series will be complete with a ten-film run over twenty years.

4. Ussher, *Fantasies of Femininity*.

5. Burgess and Gold, *Geography, the Media, and Popular Culture*, 1.

6. Lefebvre, *Production of Space*.

7. Plesnar, "Represented Space in Film."

8. Cresswell and Dixon, "Engaging Film," 1.

9. Beltrán, "New Hollywood Racelessness."

10. Bray, "Fast and Furious," para. 3.

11. Koehler, "Fast Five," para. 2.

12. L'Pree, "Race and Gender," para. 3.

13. Woolf, *A Room of One's Own*, 74–75.

14. Steiger, "No Clean Slate," 104.

15. Ulaby, "Bechdel Rule," para. 7.

16. A microaggression is when an indirect or subtle incident discriminates against a marginalized group. For instance, the use of the word "balls" is seen as a positive attribute that men would possess. In contrast, use of the word "pussy" connotes weakness.

17. Tasker, *Spectacular Bodies*.

18. Pinedo, "Recreational Terror," 6.

19. Yet another reference to women as cars.

20. Ben-Zeev et al., "Hypermasculinity in the Media," 54.

21. Gradient Lair, "Fast and Furious 6," para. 3.

22. Gradient Lair, "Fast and Furious 6," para. 8.

23. Beltrán, "New Hollywood Racelessness."

24. Beltrán, "New Hollywood Racelessness," 50.

25. Beltrán, "New Hollywood Racelessness."

26. Beltrán, "New Hollywood Racelessness," 53.

27. Beltrán, "New Hollywood Racelessness."
28. Beltrán, "New Hollywood Racelessness."
29. Beltrán, "New Hollywood Racelessness," 50.
30. Beltrán, "New Hollywood Racelessness," 59.

3. SCARED TO DEATH

1. M. England, "Breached Bodies and Home Invasions."
2. Clover, *Men, Women, and Chainsaws*; M. England, "Breached Bodies and Home Invasions"; Schoell, *Stay Out of the Shower*.
3. Clover, *Men, Women, and Chainsaws*, 36.
4. M. England, "Breached Bodies and Home Invasions."
5. Harris, "Japanese Horror Films," n.p.
6. Tadayuki, "Interview with Hideo Nakata," n.p.
7. Uyemura, "The Horror."
8. Uyemura, "The Horror."
9. Tadayuki, "Interview with Hideo Nakata," n.p.
10. Kristeva, *Powers of Horror*.
11. Cresswell, *In Place/Out of Place*; Rose, *Feminism and Geography*; Sibley, *Geographies of Exclusion*.
12. Grosz, *Volatile Bodies*, 192.
13. M. England, "Breached Bodies and Home Invasions."
14. Creed, *Monstrous-Feminine*, 10.
15. Douglas, *Purity and Danger*, 121.
16. Huggan, "Ghost Stories," 353–54.
17. Kalat, *J-Horror*, 14.
18. Sobchack, "Bringing It All Back Home," 145.
19. Sobchack, "Bringing It All Back Home," 145.
20. M. England, "Breached Bodies and Home Invasions."
21. Sobchack, "Bringing It All Back Home," 147.
22. Tadayuki, "Interview with Hideo Nakata," n.p.
23. Tadayuki, "Interview with Hideo Nakata."
24. Quote from website http://www.utusan.com,accessed May 24, 2006. No longer available.

4. VISIONS OF GENDER

1. Wills, "Modes of Production."
2. Duncan, *BodySpace*.
3. Rose, *Feminism and Geography*.
4. Massey, "Politics and Space/Time."

5. Massey, "Politics and Space/Time."
6. Rose, *Feminism and Geography*.
7. Duncan, *BodySpace*.
8. Gutmann, *Meanings of Macho*.
9. Duncan, *BodySpace*.
10. Condit, "Rhetorical Limits of Polysemy."
11. Condit, "Rhetorical Limits of Polysemy."
12. Radcliffe and Westwood, *Remaking the Nation*.
13. Rose, *Feminism and Geography*.
14. Brunsdon and Spigel, *Feminist Television Criticism*.
15. Dow, *Prime-Time Feminism*, xviii.
16. D'Acci, *Defining Women*.
17. S. Douglas, *Where the Girls Are*.
18. Bowlby, Foord, and McDowell, "Place of Gender in Locality Studies."
19. S. Douglas, *Where the Girls Are*.
20. S. Douglas, *Where the Girls Are*.
21. Waters and Huck, "Networking Women."
22. Rowe, *Unruly Women*.
23. Press, *Women Watching TV*.
24. Rose, *Feminism and Geography*.
25. de Beauvoir, *Second Sex*.
26. de Beauvoir, *Second Sex*.
27. Dow, *Prime-Time Feminism*.
28. Dow, *Prime-Time Feminism*.
29. Dow, *Prime-Time Feminism*.
30. Dow, *Prime-Time Feminism*.
31. Dow, *Prime-Time Feminism*.
32. Seiter, *Remote Control*.

5. NAVIGATING DEGRASSI COMMUNITY SCHOOL

1. Byers, "Education and Entertainment."
2. Rintoul and Hewlett, "Negotiating Canadian Culture," note 1.
3. Rintoul and Hewlett, "Negotiating Canadian Culture," 126–27.
4. Lefebvre, "Adolescence through the Looking-Glass," 84–85.
5. Lefebvre, "Adolescence through the Looking-Glass," 96.
6. Byers, "Education and Entertainment," 196.
7. Lefebvre, "Adolescence through the Looking-Glass," 95.
8. Weller, "Situating (Young) Teenagers."
9. N. Adams, "Sad Turn," para. 9.

10. N. Adams, "Sad Turn," para. 10.

11. Wilford, "Sixteen Times," para. 2.

12. Schwartzberg, "Real Teens, Real Issues," para. 2.

7. KINKY GEOGRAPHIES

1. Kendrick, *Secret Museum*.

2. Dworkin, "Erotica and Grief"; Dworkin, "Against the Male Flood"; MacKinnon, *Feminism Unmodified*; MacKinnon, "Only Words."

3. McElroy, "Liberal Feminism"; McElroy, "Individualist Feminism"; Strossen, *Defending Erotica*.

4. Califia, *Public Sex*; Queen, *Real Live Nude Girl*; Rubin, "Thinking Sex."

5. Kipnis, *Ecstasy Unlimited*, 221.

6. See Papayanis, "Sex and the Revanchist City," and Zook, "Underground Globalization," as exceptions.

7. Williams, *Porn Studies*, 2.

8. Williams, *Porn Studies*.

9. Binnie, "Erotic Possibilities of the City," 109.

10. Kroll, *Complete Reprint of Bizarre*, 6.

11. Pine, "*Bizarre* Fashion," 10.

12. Pine, "*Bizarre* Fashion."

13. Pine, "*Bizarre* Fashion."

14. Pine, "*Bizarre* Fashion," 15.

15. Pine, "*Bizarre* Fashion," 6.

16. Kroll, *Complete Reprint of Bizarre*.

17. Pine, "*Bizarre* Fashion."

18. Steele, *Fetish*, n.p.

19. Steele, *Fetish*.

20. Foucault, *History of Sexuality*, 292.

21. Pine, "Bizarre Fashion," 1.

22. Steele, *Fetish*, n.p.

23. Steele, *Fetish*, n.p.

24. Hamlyn, "Freud, Fabric, Fetish," 12.

25. Pine, "*Bizarre* Fashion," 19.

26. Secor, "Veil and Urban Space in Istanbul," 8.

27. Secor, "Veil and Urban Space in Istanbul."

28. Steele, *Fetish*, n.p.

29. Steele, *Fetish*, n.p.

30. Steele, *Fetish*, n.p.

31. Steele, *Fetish*, n.p.

32. Steele, *Fetish*, n.p.
33. Pine, "*Bizarre* Fashion."
34. Pine, "*Bizarre* Fashion," 2.
35. Pine, "*Bizarre* Fashion."
36. Pine, "*Bizarre* Fashion," figs. 9–10.
37. Kroll, *Complete Reprint of Bizarre*, 11.
38. Stryker, "Kitty Stryker."
39. Stryker, "A Little Story," paras. 3–4.
40. Stryker, "50 Shades," para. 5.
41. Stryker, "50 Shades," para. 5.
42. Stryker, "50 Shades," para. 13.
43. Stryker, "Public Kink!," para. 1.
44. Stryker, "Public Kink!," paras. 3–4.
45. Stryker, "Public Kink," para. 6.
46. Anderson, *Imagined Communities*.
47. Anderson, *Imagined Communities*.
48. Stryker, "Community," paras. 4–5.
49. Pine, "*Bizarre* Fashion," 21.
50. Pine, "*Bizarre* Fashion," 22.
51. Pine, "*Bizarre* Fashion," 30.
52. Stryker, "Andro-Aperture Project," para. 2.
53. Stryker, "Andro-Aperture Project," para. 5.

Bibliography

Adams, Nick. "Sad Turn for Adam on *Degrassi* in Last Night's Episode." August 16, 2013. http://www.glaad.org/blog/sad-turn-adam-degrassi-last-nights-episode -spoiler.

Adams, Paul C. "Television as Gathering Place." *Annals of the Association of American Geographers* 82, no. 1 (1992): 117–35.

Anderson, Benedict. *Imagined Communities: Reflections on the Origin and Spread of Nationalism*. New York: Verso, 2006.

Ardener, Shirley. *Women and Space: Ground Rules and Social Maps*. Oxford: Berg, 1993.

Auerbach, Nina. *Our Vampires, Ourselves*. Chicago: University of Chicago Press, 1995.

Aurthur, Kate. "Television's Most Persistent Taboo." *New York Times*, July 18, 2004.

Baumer, Terry. "Research on Fear of Crime in the United States." *Victimology* 3, no. 3–4 (1978): 254–64.

Bell, David. "Pleasure and Danger: The Paradoxical Spaces of Sexual Citizenship." *Political Geography* 14, no. 2 (1995): 139–53.

Ben-Zeev, Avi, Liz Scharnetzki, Lann K. Chan, and Tara C. Dennehy. "Hypermasculinity in the Media: When Men "Walk into the Fog" to Avoid Affective Communication." *Psychology of Popular Media Culture* 1, no. 1 (2012): 53–61.

Beltrán, Mary C. "The New Hollywood Racelessness: Only the Fast, Furious, (and Multiracial) Will Survive." *Cinema Journal* 44, no. 2 (2005): 50–67.

Berg, Lawrence D., and Robyn Longhurst. "Placing Masculinities and Geography." *Gender, Place, and Culture* 10, no. 4 (2003): 351–60.

Binnie, Jon. "The Erotic Possibilities of the City." In *Pleasure Zones: Bodies, Cities,*

Spaces, edited by David Bell, Jon Binnie, Ruth Holliday, Robyn Longhurst, and Robin Peace, 103–28. Syracuse NY: Syracuse University Press, 2001.

Bondi, Liz. "Gender, Class, and Urban Space: Public and Private Space in Contemporary Urban Landscapes." *Urban Geography* 19, no. 2 (1998): 160–85.

Bondi, Liz, and Mona Domosh. "On the Contours of Public Space: A Tale of Three Women." *Antipode* 30, no. 3 (1998): 270–89.

Bowlby, Sophie R., Jo Foord, and Linda McDowell. "The Place of Gender in Locality Studies." *Area* 18, no. 4 (1986): 327–31.

Boyer, Kate. "Place and the Politics of Virtue: Clerical Work, Corporate Anxiety, and Changing Meanings of Public Womanhood in Early Twentieth-Century Montreal." *Gender, Place, and Culture* 5, no. 3 (1998): 261–76.

Braidotti, Rosa. "The Politics of Ontological Differences." In *Between Feminism and Psychoanalysis,* edited by Teresa Brennan, 89–105. London: Routledge, 1989.

Bray, Catherine. "Fast and Furious." *Film4,* July 5, 2011. http://www.film4.com/reviews/2011/fast-furious-5.

Brown, Mary Ellen, ed. *Television and Women's Culture: The Politics of the Popular.* London: Sage, 1989.

Brown, Michael P. *Closet Space: Geographies of Metaphor from the Body to the Globe.* London: Routledge, 2000.

Brunsdon, Charlotte, and Lynn Spigel, eds. *Feminist Television Criticism: A Reader.* London: McGraw-Hill (UK), 2007.

Burgess, Jacquelin. "Focusing on Fear: The Use of Focus Groups in a Project for the Community Forest Unit, Countryside Commission." *Area* 28, no. 2 (1996): 130–35.

Burgess, Jacquelin, and John R. Gold, eds. *Geography, the Media, and Popular Culture.* London: Croom Helm, 1985.

Butler, Ruth E., and Sophie Bowlby. "Bodies and Spaces: An Exploration of Disabled People's Experiences of Public Space." *Environment and Planning D: Society and Space* 15, no. 4 (1997): 411–33.

Byers, Michele. "Education and Entertainment: The Many Reals of *Degrassi*." *Programming Reality: Perspectives on English-Canadian Television* (2008): 187–204.

Califia, Pat. *Public Sex: The Culture of Radical Sex.* San Francisco: Cleis, 1994.

Carey, James W. *Communication as Culture: Essays on Media and Society.* Boston: Unwin Hyman, 1998.

Carroll, Noel. *The Philosophy of Horror: Or, Paradoxes of the Heart.* London: Routledge, 2003.

Chapkis, Wendy. *Live Sex Acts: Women Performing Erotic Labor.* London: Routledge, 1997.

Clover, Carol. *Men, Women, and Chainsaws*. Princeton NJ: Princeton University Press, 1994.

Condit, Celeste. "The Rhetorical Limits of Polysemy." *Critical Studies in Mass Communication* 6, no. 2 (1989): 103–22.

Corner, John. *Critical Ideas in Television Studies*. Oxford: Oxford University Press, 1999.

Craine, James W. "Virtualizing Los Angeles: Pierre Levy, *The Shield*, and theshieldfans .com." Paper presented at the Annual Meeting of the Association of American Geographers, Chicago IL, March 2006.

Creed, Barbara. *The Monstrous-Feminine: Film, Feminism, Psychoanalysis*. London: Routledge, 1993.

Cresswell, Tim. *In Place/Out of Place*. Minneapolis: University of Minnesota Press, 1996.

Cresswell, Tim, and Deborah Dixon. "Introduction: Engaging Film." In *Engaging Film: Geographies of Mobility and Identity*, edited by Tim Cresswell and Deborah Dixon, 1–10. Lanham MD: Rowman and Littlefield, 2002.

D'Acci, Julie. *Defining Women: Television and the Case of Cagney and Lacey*. Chapel Hill: University of North Carolina Press, 1994.

Day, Kristen. "Better Safe Than Sorry? Consequences of Sexual Assault Prevention for Women in Public Space." *Perspectives on Social Problems* 9 (1997): 83–101.

——— . "Constructing Masculinity and Women's Fear in Public Space in Irvine, California." *Gender, Place, and Culture* 8, no. 2 (2001): 109–27.

——— . "Embassies and Sanctuaries: Women's Experiences of Race and Fear in Public Space." *Environment and Planning D: Society and Space* 17, no. 3 (1999): 307–28.

de Beauvoir, Simone. *The Second Sex*, translated by H. M. Parshley. London: Picador, 1988.

Derrida, Jacques. *Dissemination*, translated by Barbara Johnson. Chicago: University of Chicago Press, 1983.

Douglas, Mary. *Purity and Danger*. London: Ark, 1984.

Douglas, Susan J. *Where the Girls Are: Growing Up Female with the Mass Media*. New York: Random House, 1994.

Dow, Bonnie J. *Prime-Time Feminism: Television, Media, Culture, and the Women's Movement Since 1970*. Philadelphia: University of Pennsylvania Press, 1996.

Duncan, Nancy, ed. *BodySpace: Destabilizing Geographies of Gender and Sexuality*. London: Routledge, 1996.

Dworkin, Andrea. "Against the Male Flood: Censorship, Erotica, and Equality." In *Feminism and Erotica*, edited by Drucilla Cornell, 19–38. Oxford: Oxford University Press, 2000.

———. "Erotica and Grief." In *Feminism and Erotica*, edited by Drucilla Cornell, 39–44. Oxford: Oxford University Press, 2000.

England, Kim. "Gender Relations and the Spatial Structure of the City." *Geoforum* 22, no. 2 (1991): 135–47.

England, Marcia. "Breached Bodies and Home Invasions: Horrific Representations of the Feminized Body and Home." *Gender, Place, and Culture* 13, no. 4 (2006): 353–63.

England, Marcia R., and Stephanie Simon. "Scary Cities: Urban Geographies of Fear, Difference, and Belonging: Editorial." *Social and Cultural Geography* 11, no. 3 (2010): 201–207.

Fiske, John. *Reading the Popular*. Boston: Unwin Hyman, 1989.

———. *Television Culture*. London: Methuen, 1987.

———. *Understanding Popular Culture*. Boston: Unwin Hyman, 1989.

Foucault, Michel. *The History of Sexuality: An Introduction*. New York: Vintage Books, 1990.

Gelder, Ken. "Introduction: The Field of Horror." In *The Horror Reader*, edited by Ken Gelder, 1–7. London: Routledge, 2000.

Gerbner, George, and Larry Gross. "Living with Television: The Violence Profile." *Journal of Communication* 26, no. 2 (1976): 172–99.

Golden, Christopher, and Nancy Holder. *The Watcher's Guide*. New York: Pocket Books, 1998.

Gordon, Joan, and Veronica Hollinger. "Introduction: The Shape of Vampires." In *Blood Read: The Vampire as Metaphor in Contemporary Culture*, edited by Joan Gordon and Veronica Hollinger, 1–7. Philadelphia: University of Pennsylvania Press, 1997.

Gordon, Margaret T., and Stephanie Riger. *The Female Fear*. Chicago: University of Illinois Press, 1991.

Gradient Lair. "*Fast & Furious 6*: Colourism, Race, and Stereotypes." 2013. http://www .gradientlair.com/post/54196864103/fast-and-furious-6-colourism-race -stereotypes.

Granello, Darcy Haag. "Using *Beverly Hills, 90210* to Explore Developmental Issues in Female Adolescents." *Youth and Society* 29, no 1 (1997): 24–54.

Green, Phillip. *Cracks in the Pedestal: Ideology and Gender in Hollywood*. Amherst: University of Massachusetts Press, 1998.

Gregory, Derek. *Geographical Imaginations*. Malden MA: Wiley-Blackwell, 1994.

Grosz, Elizabeth. *Volatile Bodies: Toward a Corporeal Feminism*. Bloomington: Indiana University Press, 1994.

Gutmann, Matthew C. *The Meanings of Macho: Being a Man in Mexico City*. Berkeley: University of California Press, 1996.

Hall, Stuart. "The Whites of Their Eyes: Racist Ideologies and the Media." In *Gender, Race, and Class in Media: A Text-Reader*, edited by Gail Dines and Jean M. Humez, 18–22. Thousand Oaks CA: Sage, 1995.

Hamlyn, Anne. "Freud, Fabric, Fetish." *Textile* 1, no. 1 (2003): 8–26.

Hansen, Mark B. N. "Affect as Medium, or the 'Digital-Facial-Image.'" *Journal of Visual Culture* 2, no. 2 (2003): 205–28.

Haraway, Donna. "Situated Knowledges: The Science Question in Feminism and the Privilege of Partial Perspective." *Feminist Studies* 14, no. 3 (1988): 575–600.

Harris, Mark. "Japanese Horror Films: Beasts from the Far East." October 30, 2015. https://www.thoughtco.com/japanese-horror-movies-1872928.

Harvey, David. "On the History and Present Condition of Geography: An Historical Materialist Manifesto." *Professional Geographer* 36, no. 1 (1984): 1–11.

———. *Social Justice and the City*. Baltimore MD: The John Hopkins University Press, 1973.

Hollinger, Veronica. "Fantasies of Absence: The Postmodern Vampire." In *Blood Read: The Vampire as Metaphor in Contemporary Culture*, edited by Joan Gordon and Veronica Hollinger, 199–212. Philadelphia: University of Pennsylvania Press, 1997.

Huggan, Graham. "Ghost Stories, Bone Flutes, Contemporary Cannibalism." In *The Horror Reader*, edited by Ken Gelder, 352–63. London: Routledge, 2000.

Jackson, Peter. "The Cultural Politics of Masculinity: Towards a Social Geography." *Transactions of the Institute of British Geographers* 16, no. 2 (1991): 199–213.

Jarosz, Lucy A. "Agents of Power, Landscapes of Fear: The Vampires and Heart Thieves of Madagascar." *Environment and Planning D: Society and Space* 12, no. 4 (1994): 421–36.

Kalat, David. *J-Horror: The Definitive Guide to* The Ring, The Grudge, *and Beyond*. New York: Vertical, 2007.

Kaviraj, Sudipta. "Filth and the Public Sphere: Concepts and Practices about Space in Calcutta." *Public Culture* 10, no. 1 (1997): 83–113.

Kellner, Douglas. "Cultural Studies, Multiculturalism, and Media Culture." In *Gender, Race, and Class in Media: A Text Reader*, edited by Gail Dines and Jean M. Humez, 9–20. Thousand Oaks CA: Sage, 1995.

———. "TV, Ideology, and Emancipatory Popular Culture." In *Television: The Critical View*, edited by Horace Newcomb, 471–503. Oxford: Oxford University Press, 1987.

Kendrick, Walter. *The Secret Museum: Erotica in Modern Culture*. New York: Viking, 1987.

Kern, Leslie. "Selling the 'Scary City': Gendering Freedom, Fear, and Condominium Development in the Neoliberal City." *Social and Cultural Geography* 11, no. 3 (2010): 209–30.

Kilian, Ted. "Public and Private, Power and Space." In *Philosophy and Geography II: The Production of Public Space*, edited by Andrew Light and Jonathan M. Smith, 115–34. Lanham MD: Rowman and Littlefield, 1998.

Kipnis, Laura. *Ecstasy Unlimited: On Sex, Capital, Gender, and Aesthetics*. Minneapolis: University of Minnesota Press, 1993.

Kitchin, Robert M. "Towards Geographies of Cyberspace." *Progress in Human Geography* 22, no. 3 (1998): 385–406.

Koehler, Robert. "Fast Five." *Variety*, April 21, 2011. http://www.variety.com/review/VE1117945052?refcatid=31.

Koskela, Hille. "Bold Walk and Breakings: Women's Spatial Confidence Versus Fear of Violence." *Gender, Place, and Culture* 4, no. 3 (1997): 301–20.

Kristeva, Julia. *Powers of Horror: An Essay on Abjection*. New York: Columbia University Press, 1982.

Kroll, Eric. *The Complete Reprint of John Willie's* Bizarre. Mishawaka IN: Better World Books, 1996.

Lee, Janet. "Subversive Sitcoms: *Roseanne* as an Inspiration for Feminist Resistance." In *Gender, Race, and Class in Media: A Text Reader*, edited by Gale Dines and Jean M. Humez, 469–75. Thousand Oaks CA: Sage, 1995.

Lefebvre, Benjamin. "Adolescence through the Looking-Glass: Ideology and the Represented Child in *Degrassi: The Next Generation*." *Canadian Children's Literature* [*Littérature canadienne pour la jeunesse*] 33, no. 1 (2009): 82–106.

Lefebvre, Henri. *The Production of Space*. Oxford: Blackwell, 1991.

Levy, Pierre. *Becoming Virtual: Reality in the Digital Age*. New York: Plenum Trade, 1998.

Lindlof, Thomas R. *Qualitative Communication Research Methods*. Thousand Oaks CA: Sage, 1995.

Livingstone, Sonia. "Mediated Knowledge: Recognition of the Familiar, Discovery of the New." In *Television and Common Knowledge*, edited by Jostein Gripsrud, 97–107. London: Routledge, 1999.

Longhurst, Robin. "The Body and Geography." *Gender, Place, and Culture* 2, no. 1 (1995): 97–105.

———. "(Dis)embodied Geographies." *Progress in Human Geography* 21, no. 4 (1997): 486–501.

L'Pree, Charisse. "Race and Gender in the Fast and Furious Franchise." December 1, 2013.

https://charisselpree.com/2013/12/01/race-and-gender-in-the-fast-and-furious
-franchise/.

Lull, James. "How Families Select T V Programs: A Mass Observational Study." *Journal of Broadcasting* 26, no. 4 (1982): 801–11.

MacDonald, Myra. *Representing Women: Myths of Femininity in the Popular Media.* London: Arnold, 1995.

Macek, Steve. *Urban Nightmares: The Media, the Right, and the Moral Panic over the City.* Minneapolis: University of Minnesota Press, 2006.

MacKinnon, Catharine. *Feminism Unmodified.* Cambridge M A : Harvard University Press, 1987.

———. "Only Words." In *Feminism and Erotica*, edited by Drucilla Cornell, 94–120. Oxford: Oxford University Press, 2000.

Marston, Sallie. "The Private Goes Public: Citizenship and the New Spaces of Civil Society." *Political Geography* 14, no. 2 (1995): 194–98.

Massey, Doreen. "The Geographical Mind." In *Secondary Geography Handbook*, edited by David Balderson, 46–61. Sheffield UK: Geographical Association, 2006.

———. "In Public: The Street and Places of Pleasure." In *Gender, Identity, and Place: Understanding Feminist Geographies*, edited by Linda McDowell, 148–69. Minneapolis: University of Minnesota Press, 1999.

———. "Politics and Space/Time." *New Left Review* 196 (1992): 65–84.

McDowell, Linda, ed. *Gender, Identity, and Place: Understanding Feminist Geographies.* Minneapolis: University of Minnesota Press, 1999.

McElroy, Wendy. "Individualist Feminism: A True Defense of Erotica." In *Contemporary Moral Issues*, edited by W. S. Cragg and C. M. Koggel, 220–21. Toronto: McGraw-Hill Ryerson, 1997.

———. "Liberal Feminism: The Glimmer of Hope." In *Contemporary Moral Issues*, edited by W. S. Cragg and C. M. Koggel, 216–19. Toronto: McGraw-Hill Ryerson, 1997.

Meyrowitz, Joshua. *No Sense of Place: The Impact of Electronic Media on Social Behavior.* Oxford: Oxford University Press, 1985.

Moretti, Franco. "A Capital Dracula." In *Dracula: Authoritative Text, Contexts, Reviews and Reactions, Dramatic and Film Variations, Criticism*, edited by Nina Auerbach and David J. Skal, 431–44. New York: W. W. Norton, 1997.

Morley, David. *Television, Audiences, and Cultural Studies.* London: Routledge, 1992.

Nast, Heidi, and Steve Pile. *Places Through the Body.* London: Routledge, 1998.

Owen, Susan. "Buffy the Vampire Slayer: Vampires, Postmodernity, and Postfeminism." *Journal of Popular Film and Television* 27, no. 2 (1999): 24–31.

Pain, Rachel. "The Geography of Fear." *Geography Review* 12, no. 5 (1999): 22–25.

―――. "Space, Sexual Violence, and Social Control: Integrating Geographical and Feminist Analyses of Women's Fear of Crime." *Progress in Human Geography* 15, no. 4 (1991): 415–31.

Papayanis, Marilyn Adler. "Sex and the Revanchist City: Zoning Out Pornography in New York." *Environment and Planning D: Society and Space* 18, no. 3 (2000): 341–52.

Pile, Steve. *The Body and the City: Psychoanalysis, Space, and Subjectivity*. Florence KY: Psychology Press of Routledge's Taylor and Francis Group, 1996.

Pine, Julia. "In *Bizarre* Fashion: The Double-Voiced Discourse of John Willie's Fetish Fantasia." *Journal of the History of Sexuality* 22, no. 1 (2013): 1–33.

Pinedo, Isabel Cristina. *Recreational Terror: Women and the Pleasure of Horror Film Viewing*. Albany: State University of New York Press, 1997.

Plesnar, Lukasz. "Represented Space in Film." In *The Jagiellonian University Film Studies*, edited by Wieslaw Godzic. Krakow: Universitas, 1996.

Press, Andrea L. *Women Watching TV: Gender, Class, and Generation in the American Television Experience*. Philadelphia: University of Pennsylvania Press, 1991.

Queen, Carol. *Real Live Nude Girl: Chronicles of Sex-Positive Culture*. Pittsburgh PA: Cleis Press, 1997.

Radcliffe, Sarah, and Sallie Westwood. *Remaking the Nation: Place, Identity, and Politics in Latin America*. London: Routledge, 1996.

Rath, Claus-Dieter. "Live Television and Its Audiences: Challenges of Media Reality." In *Remote Control: Television, Audiences, and Cultural Power*, edited by Ellen Seiter, Hans Borchers, Gabrielle Kreutzner, and Eva-Maria Warth, 79–95. London: Routledge, 1989.

Rintoul, Suzanne, and Quintin Zachary Hewlett. "Negotiating Canadian Culture through Youth Television: Discourse on *Degrassi*." *Jeunesse: Young People, Texts, Cultures* 1, no. 1 (2009): 125–47.

Risman, Barbara J. *Gender Vertigo: American Families in Transition*. New Haven CT: Yale University Press, 1999.

Rose, Gillian. *Feminism and Geography: The Limits of Geographical Knowledge*. Minneapolis: University of Minnesota Press, 1993.

―――. *Visual Methodologies: An Introduction to Researching with Visual Materials*. Thousand Oaks CA: Sage, 2001.

Rowe, Kathleen. "Roseanne: Unruly Woman as Domestic Goddess." In *Feminist Television Criticism: A Reader*, edited by Charlotte Brunsdon, Julie D'Acci, and Lynn Spigel, 74–83. Oxford: Clarendon Press, 1997.

―――. *The Unruly Women: Gender and the Genres of Laughter*. Austin: University of Texas Press, 1995.

Rubin, Gayle. "Thinking Sex: Notes for a Radical Theory of the Politics of Sexuality."

In *Pleasure and Danger: Exploring Female Sexuality*, edited by Carol S. Vance, 267–319. London: Routledge, 1984.

Schaffer, Talia. "A Wilde Desire: The Homoerotic History of Dracula." In *Dracula: Authoritative Text, Contexts, Reviews and Reactions, Dramatic and Film Variations, Criticism*, edited by Nina Auerbach and David J. Skal, 470–82. New York: W. W. Norton, 1997.

Schoell, William. *Stay Out of the Shower: 25 Years of Shocker Films, Beginning with Psycho*. New York: Dembner Books, 1985.

Schwartzberg, Shlomo. "Real Teens, Real Issues: TV's *Degrassi*." July 15, 2011. http://www.criticsatlarge.ca/2011/07/real-teens-real-issues-tvs-degrassi.html.

Secor, Anna J. "The Veil and Urban Space in Istanbul: Women's Dress, Mobility and Islamic Knowledge." *Gender, Place, and Culture: A Journal of Feminist Geography* 9, no. 1 (2002): 5–22.

Seiter, Ellen, ed. *Remote Control: Television, Audiences, and Cultural Power*. London: Routledge, 1989.

Senf, Carol A. "Dracula: The Unseen Face in the Mirror." In *Dracula: Authoritative Text, Contexts, Reviews and Reactions, Dramatic and Film Variations, Criticism*, edited by Nina Auerbach and David J. Skal, 421–31. New York: W. W. Norton, 1997.

Sennett, Richard. *Flesh and Stone: The Body and the City in Western Civilization*. New York: W. W. Norton, 1994.

Sibley, David. *Geographies of Exclusion*. London: Routledge, 1995.

Simonetti, Marie-Claire. "Teenage Truths and Tribulations Across Cultures: *Degrassi Junior High* and *Beverly Hills, 90210*." *Journal of Popular Film and Television* 22, no. 1 (1994): 38–42.

Smith, Susan J. "Fear of Crime: Beyond a Geography of Deviance." *Progress in Human Geography* 11, no. 1 (1987): 1–23.

Sobchack, Vivian. "Bringing It All Back Home: Family Economy and Generic Exchange." In *Dread of Difference: Gender and the Horror Film*, edited by Barry Keith Grant. Austin: University of Texas Press, 1996.

Spain, Daphne. *Gendered Spaces*. Chapel Hill: University of North Carolina Press, 1992.

Staeheli, Lynn. "Publicity, Privacy, and Women's Political Action." *Environment and Planning D: Society and Space* 14, no. 5 (1996): 601–19.

Stanko, Elizabeth. *Everyday Violence: How Women and Men Experience Sexual and Physical Danger*. London: Pandora Press, 1990.

———. "Ordinary Fear: Women, Violence, and Personal Safety." In *Violence Against Women: The Bloody Footprints*, edited by Paula Bart and Eileen Moran, 155–64. Thousand Oaks CA: Sage, 1993.

Steele, Valerie. *Fetish: Fashion, Sex, and Power*. Oxford: Oxford University Press, 1995.

Steiger, Kay. "No Clean Slate: Unshakable Race and Gender Politics in *The Walking Dead*." In *Triumph of* The Walking Dead: *Robert Kirkman's Zombie Epic on Page and Screen*, edited by James Lowder. Dallas: Smart Pop, 2011.

Stoker, Bram. *Dracula: A Norton Critical Edition*, edited by Nina Auerbach and David J. Skal. New York: W. W. Norton, 1997.

Strong-Boag, Veronica, Isabel Dyck, Kim England, and Louise Johnson. "What Women's Spaces? Women in Australian, British, Canadian, and U.S. Suburbs." In *Changing Suburbs: Foundation, Form, and Function*, edited by Richard Harris and Peter J. Larkham, 168–86. London: Chapman and Hall, 1999.

Strossen, Nadine. *Defending Erotica: Free Speech, Sex, and the Fight for Women's Rights*. New York: New York University Press, 2000.

Stryker, Miss Kitty. "50 Shades of Fucked Up: How BDSM in Film Fails Everyone." *Kitty Stryker: The Most Dangerous Liaison*. July 28, 2014. http://kittystryker .com/blog/posts/50-shades-of-fucked-up-how-bdsm-in-film-fails-everyone/.

———. "The Andro-Apeture Project." *Kitty Stryker: The Most Dangerous Liaison*. June 20, 2011. http://kittystryker.com/blog/posts/the-andro-aperture-project/.

———. "Community—And I Don't Mean the TV Show." *Kitty Stryker: The Most Dangerous Liaison*. November 13, 2015. http://kittystryker.com/blog/posts /community/.

———. "A Little Story about Bondage." *Kitty Stryker: The Most Dangerous Liaison*. October 7, 2016. http://kittystryker.com/blog/posts/a-little-story-about -bondage/.

———. "Kitty Stryker: The Most Dangerous Liaison." 2017. http://kittystryker .com/blog.

———. "Public Kink!=LGBT Rights." *Kitty Stryker: The Most Dangerous Liaison*. August 24, 2011. http://kittystryker.com/blog/posts/public-kink-lgbt-rights/.

Tadayuki, Naito. "Interview with Hideo Nakata, Specter Director." *Kateigaho* (Winter 2005). http://int.kateigaho.com/win05/horror-nakata.html.

Tasker, Yvonne. *Spectacular Bodies: Gender, Genre, and the Action Cinema*. London: Routledge, 2012.

Taylor, Ella. *Prime Time Families: Television Culture in Postwar America*. Berkeley: University of California Press, 1989.

Thompson, John B. "Social Theory and the Media." In *Communication Theory Today*, edited by David Crowley and David Mitchell, 27–49. Stanford: Stanford University Press, 1994.

Tracy, Kathleen. *The Girl's Got Bite: The Unofficial Guide to Buffy's World*. Los Angeles: Renaissance, 1998.

Trinta, Aluizio R. "News from Home: A Study of Realism and Melodrama in Brazilian

Telenovelas." In *The Television Studies Book*, edited by Christine Geraghty and David Lusted, 275–85. London: Arnold, 1998.

Ulaby, Neda. "The 'Bechdel Rule': Defining Pop-Culture Character." September 2, 2008. http://www.npr.org/templates/story/story.php?storyId=94202522.

Ussher, Jane M. *Fantasies of Femininity: Reframing the Boundaries of Sex*. London: Penguin, 1997.

Uyemura, Kristin. "The Horror." January 9, 2006. http://the.honoluluadvertiser.com/article/2006/Jan/09/il/FP601090314.html.

Vaiou, Dina. "Gender Divisions in Urban Space: Beyond the Rigidity of Dualist Classifications." *Antipode* 24, no. 4 (1992): 247–62.

Valentine, Gill. "The Body." In *Social Geographies: Space and Society*, edited by Gill Valentine, 15–62. London: Prentice Hall, 2000.

———. "The Geography of Women's Fear." *Area* 21, no. 4 (1989): 385–90.

———. "Images of Danger: Women's Sources of Information about the Spatial Distribution of Male Violence." *Area* 24, no. 1 (1992): 22–29.

———. "London's Streets of Fear." In *The Crisis of London*, edited by Andrew Thornely, 90–102. London: Routledge, 1992.

———. "Women's Fear and the Design of Public Space." *Built Environment* 16, no. 4 (1990): 288–303.

van Dijk, J. J. M. "Public Attitudes toward Crime in the Netherlands." *Victimology* 3, no. 3–4 (1978): 265–73.

Warr, Mark. "Fear of Rape among Urban Women." *Social Problems* 32, no. 3 (1985): 238–50.

Waters, Harry F., and Janet Huck. "Networking Women." *Newsweek*, March 13, 1989.

Wekerle, Gerda R., and Carolyn Whitzman. *Safe Cities*. New York: Van Nostrand Reinhold, 1994.

Weller, Susie. "Situating (Young) Teenagers in Geographies of Children and Youth." *Children's Geographies* 4, no. 1 (2006): 97–108.

Wilford, Denette. "Sixteen Times *Degrassi* Totally Nailed What It's Like to Be a Teenager." October 27, 2013. http://www.theloop.ca/16-times-degrassi-totally-nailed-what-its-like-to-be-a-teenager/.

Williams, Linda, ed. *Porn Studies*. Durham NC: Duke University Press, 2004.

Wills, Jane. "Modes of Production/Modes of Reproduction." In *A Feminist Glossary of Human Geography*, edited by Linda McDowell and Joanne P. Sharp, 171. London: Arnold. 1999.

Wilson, Barbara J., Edward Donnerstein, Daniel Linz, Dale Kunkel, J. Potter, S.L. Smith, E. Blumenthal, and T. Gray. "Content Analysis of Entertainment Television: The Importance of Context." In *Television Violence and Public Policy*, edited by James T. Hamilton, 13–53. Ann Arbor: University of Michigan Press, 1998.

Wilson, Elizabeth. *The Sphinx in the City: Urban Life, the Control of Disorder, and Women*. Los Angeles: University of California Press, 1992.

Woolf, Virginia. *A Room of One's Own and Three Guineas*. Oxford: Oxford University Press, 2015.

Youngs, Martyn J. "The English Television Landscape Documentary: A Look at Granada." In *Geography, the Media, and Popular Culture*, edited by Jacquelin Burgess and John R. Gold, 144–64. London: Croom Helm, 1985.

Zook, Matthew A. "Underground Globalization: Mapping the Space of Flows of the Internet Adult Industry." *Environment and Planning A* 35, no. 7 (2003): 1261–86.

Index

The Grudge, 65, 67, 69, 72–74, 77–78